BLOOM'S

HOW TO WRITE ABOUT

Toni Morrison

ZISCA ISABEL BURTON

BLOOM'S
LITERARY CRITICISM
An imprint of Infobase Publishing

Bloom's How to Write about Toni Morrison

Copyright © 2008, Zisca Burton

Bloom's Literary Criticism
An imprint of Infobase Publishing
132 West 31st Street
New York NY 10001

Library of Congress Cataloging-in-Publication Data

Burton, Zisca.
  Bloom's how to write about Toni Morrison/Zisca Burton; introduction by Harold
  Bloom.
    p. cm.
  Includes bibliographical references and index.
    ISBN 978-0-7910-9548-5 (acid-free paper) 1. Morrison, Toni—Criticism and
interpretation. 2. Criticism—Authorship. 3. Report writing. I. Bloom, Harold. II.
Title. III. Title: How to write about Toni Morrison.

  PS3563.O8749Z575 2007
  813.'54—dc22

                                                          2007008096

Chelsea House books are available at special discounts when purchased in bulk quantities for businesses, associations, institutions, or sales promotions. Please call our Special Sales Department in New York at (212) 967-8800 or (800) 322-8755.

You can find Chelsea House on the World Wide Web at http://www.chelseahouse.com

Text design by Annie O'Donnell
Cover design by Ben Peterson

Printed in the United States of America

Bang MSRF 10 9 8 7 6 5 4 3 2 1

This book is printed on acid-free paper.

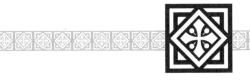

CONTENTS

SERIES
INTRODUCTION

BLOOM'S HOW to Write about Literature series is designed to inspire students to write fine essays on great writers and their works. Each volume in the series begins with an introduction by Harold Bloom, meditating on the challenges and rewards of writing about the volume's subject author. The first chapter then provides detailed instructions on how to write a good essay, including how to find a thesis; how to develop an outline; how to write a good introduction, body text, and conclusions; how to cite sources; and more. The second chapter provides a brief overview of the issues involved in writing about the subject author and then a number of suggestions for paper topics, with accompanying strategies for addressing each topic. Succeeding chapters cover the author's major works.

The paper topics suggested within this book are open-ended, and the brief strategies provided are designed to give students a push forward on the writing process rather than a road map to success. The aim of the book is to pose questions, not answer them. Many different kinds of papers could result from each topic. As always, the success of each paper will depend completely on the writer's skill and imagination.

VOLUME INTRODUCTION

by Harold Bloom

SINCE I am a kind of personalist literary critic and also am very fond of Ms. Morrison, I begin with an anecdote. Many years ago, participating in a seminar at the venerable Red Lion Inn in Stockbridge, Massachusetts, the novelist and I found ourselves trapped in its splendid late 19th-century elevator. She had earlier kindly invited me to leave the discussion and indulge in a bottle of Maker's Mark bourbon, a rather potent 100-proof whiskey. An alarmist by nature, I said to her that the elevator was our mutual doom. She heroically delivered a motherly hug (though I am older by several years) and assured me that help was on the way. A quarter-hour later, having escaped from the elevator and deep in my second glass of medicinal bourbon, I thanked her solemnly and have adored her ever since.

Her early novels, culminating in *Song of Solomon,* remain my favorites among her works, but Ms. Morrison kindly forgives me for perhaps undervaluing her fictions from *Beloved* onward. She disputes both my judgments as to the canonical and my accounts of what she regards as her own tradition. Disagreeing with a Nobel laureate is never easy, and I regard this one as a kind of icon. Nevertheless, my experience of reading her continues to see in Toni Morrison's fiction the literary ancestry of Virginia Woolf and William Faulkner and not of African-American traditions of fiction. *Beloved,* her most famous book, deliberately evokes echoes of slave narratives, yet influence can have unwilled anxieties of genealogy, and even *Beloved* has to be regarded as a daughter of Virginia Woolf and William Faulkner, in themselves a kind of unlikely union.

Still, Ms. Morrison herself linked Woolf and Faulkner in an M.A. dissertation she wrote at Cornell University. Both Faulkner and Woolf were masters of phantasmagoria, though of rather different sorts. Faulkner's *As I Lay Dying* and Woolf's *Mrs. Dalloway* seem to me their author's respective masterpieces. The violent action of Faulkner's chronicle of the Bundrens, including fire and flood, is internalized by Woolf's meditative reverie. Darl Bundren and Septimus Smith share something of a Hamlet-like madness or borderline mania, while Clarissa Dalloway wanders near a demarcation of consciousness that would ally her with both figures.

How should one write about Toni Morrison, aside from comparing her with these two prime precursors? D. H. Lawrence told us to trust the tale and not its teller. Any admirer of *Beloved* needs to organize a defense of its ghostly supernaturalism, which I myself find clashes with the brutal social realities depicted in the narrative. *Beloved* has been termed by many *the* African-American holocaust novel. That is an enormous burden for any story. Who can lift it?

HOW TO WRITE
A GOOD ESSAY

WHILE THERE are many ways to write about literature, most assignments for high school and college English classes call for analytical papers. In these assignments, you are presenting your interpretation of a text to your reader. Your objective is to interpret the text's meaning in order to enhance your reader's understanding and enjoyment of the work. Without exception, strong papers about the meaning of a literary work are built upon a careful, close reading of the text or texts. Careful, analytical reading should always be the first step in your writing process. This volume provides models of such close, analytical reading, and these should help you develop your own skills as a reader and as a writer.

As the examples throughout this book demonstrate, attentive reading entails thinking about and evaluating the formal (textual) aspects of the author's works: theme, character, form, and language. In addition, when writing about a work, many readers choose to move beyond the text itself to consider the work's cultural context. In these instances, writers might explore the historical circumstances of the time period in which the work was written. Alternatively, they might examine the philosophies and ideas that a work addresses. Even in cases where writers explore a work's cultural context, though, papers must still address the more formal aspects of the work itself. A good interpretative essay that evaluates Charles Dickens's use of the philosophy of utilitarianism in his novel *Hard Times,* for example, cannot adequately address the author's treatment of the philosophy without firmly grounding this discussion in the book itself. In other words, any analytical paper about a text, even one that seeks to evaluate the work's cultural context, must also have a

1

firm handle on the work's themes, characters, and language. You must look for and evaluate these aspects of a work, then, as you read a text and as you prepare to write about it.

WRITING ABOUT THEMES

Literary themes are more than just topics or subjects treated in a work; they are attitudes or points about these topics that often structure other elements in a work. Writing about theme therefore requires that you not just identify a topic that a literary work addresses but also discuss what that work says about that topic. For example, if you were writing about the culture of the American South in William Faulkner's famous story "A Rose for Emily," you would need to discuss what Faulkner says, argues, or implies about that culture and its passing.

When you prepare to write about thematic concerns in a work of literature, you will probably discover that, like most works of literature, your text touches upon other themes in addition to its central theme. These secondary themes also provide rich ground for paper topics. A thematic paper on "A Rose for Emily" might consider gender or race in the story. While neither of these could be said to be the central theme of the story, they are clearly related to the passing of the "old South" and could provide plenty of good material for papers.

As you prepare to write about themes in literature, you might find a number of strategies helpful. After you identify a theme or themes in the story, you should begin by evaluating how other elements of the story—such as character, point of view, imagery, and symbolism—help develop the theme. You might ask yourself what your own responses are to the author's treatment of the subject matter. Do not neglect the obvious, either: What expectations does the title set up? How does the title help develop thematic concerns? Clearly, the title "A Rose for Emily" says something about the narrator's attitude toward the title character, Emily Grierson, and all she represents.

WRITING ABOUT CHARACTER

Generally, characters are essential components of fiction and drama. (This is not always the case, though; Ray Bradbury's "August 2026: There

Will Come Soft Rains" is technically a story without characters, at least any human characters.) Often, you can discuss character in poetry, as in T. S. Eliot's "The Love Song of J. Alfred Prufrock" or Robert Browning's "My Last Duchess." Many writers find that analyzing character is one of the most interesting and engaging ways to work with a piece of literature and to shape a paper. After all, characters generally are human, and we all know something about being human and living in the world. While it is always important to remember that these figures are not real people but creations of the writer's imagination, it can be fruitful to begin evaluating them as you might evaluate a real person. Often you can start with your own response to a character. Did you like or dislike the character? Did you sympathize with the character? Why or why not?

Keep in mind, though, that emotional responses like these are just starting places. To truly explore and evaluate literary characters, you need to return to the formal aspects of the text and evaluate how the author has drawn these characters. The 20th-century writer E. M. Forster coined the terms *flat* characters and *round* characters. Flat characters are static, one-dimensional characters who frequently represent a particular concept or idea. In contrast, *round* characters are fully drawn and much more realistic characters who frequently change and develop over the course of a work. Are the characters you are studying flat or round? What elements of the characters lead you to this conclusion? Why might the author have drawn characters like this? How does their development affect the meaning of the work? Similarly, you should explore the techniques the author uses to develop characters. Do we hear a character's own words, or do we hear only other characters' assessments of him or her? Or, does the author use an omniscient or limited omniscient narrator to allow us access to the workings of the character's minds? If so, how does that help develop the characterization? Often you can even evaluate the narrator as a character. How trustworthy are the opinions and assessments of the narrator? You should also think about characters' names. Do they mean anything? If you encounter a hero named Sophia or Sophie, you should probably think about her wisdom (or lack thereof), since *sophia* means "wisdom" in Greek. Similarly, since the name *Sylvia*, is derived from the word *sylvan*, meaning "of the wood," you might want to evaluate that character's relationship with nature. Once again, you might look to the title of the work. Does Herman Melville's "Bartleby, the Scrivener" signal anything about Bartleby himself? Is Bartleby adequately defined by his job as scrivener? Is this part of Melville's point? Pursuing questions like these can help you develop thorough papers about characters from psychological, sociological, or more formalistic perspectives.

WRITING ABOUT FORM AND GENRE

Genre, a word derived from French, means "type" or "class." Literary genres are distinctive classes or categories of literary composition. On the most general level, literary works can be divided into the genres of drama, poetry, fiction, and essays, yet within those genres there are classifications that are also referred to as genres. Tragedy and comedy, for example, are genres of drama. Epic, lyric, and pastoral are genres of poetry. *Form,* on the other hand, generally refers to the shape or structure of a work. There are many clearly defined forms of poetry that follow specific patterns of meter, rhyme, and stanza. Sonnets, for example, are poems that follow a fixed form of 14 lines. Sonnets generally follow one of two basic sonnet forms, each with its own distinct rhyme scheme. Haiku is another example of poetic form, traditionally consisting of three unrhymed lines of five, seven, and five syllables.

While you might think that writing about form or genre might leave little room for argument, many of these forms and genres are very fluid. Remember that literature is evolving and ever changing, and so are its forms. As you study poetry, you may find that poets, especially more modern poets, play with traditional poetic forms, bringing about new effects. Similarly, dramatic tragedy was once quite narrowly defined, but over the centuries playwrights have broadened and challenged traditional definitions, changing the shape of tragedy. When Arthur Miller wrote *Death of a Salesman,* many critics challenged the idea that tragic drama could encompass a common man like Willy Loman.

Evaluating how a work of literature fits into or challenges the boundaries of its form or genre can provide you with fruitful avenues of investigation. Once again, you might find it helpful to ask why the work does or does not fit into traditional categories. Why might Miller have thought it fitting to write a tragedy of the common man? Similarly, you might compare the content or theme of a work with its form. How well do they work together? Many of Emily Dickinson's poems, for instance, follow the meter of traditional hymns. While some of her poems seem to express traditional religious doctrines, many seem to challenge or strain against traditional conceptions of God and theology. What is the effect, then, of her use of traditional hymn meter?

WRITING ABOUT LANGUAGE, SYMBOLS, AND IMAGERY

No matter what the genre, writers use words as their most basic tool. Language is the most fundamental building block of literature. It is essential that you pay careful attention to the author's language and word choice as you read, reread, and analyze a text. Imagery is language that appeals to the senses. Most commonly, imagery appeals to our sense of vision, creating a mental picture, but authors also use language that appeals to our other senses. Images can be literal or figurative. Literal images use sensory language to describe an actual thing. In the broadest terms, figurative language uses one thing to speak about something else. For example, if I call my boss a snake, I am not saying that he is literally a reptile. Instead, I am using figurative language to communicate my opinions about him. Since we think of snakes as sneaky, slimy, and sinister, I am using the concrete image of a snake to communicate these abstract opinions and impressions.

The two most common figures of speech are similes and metaphors. Both are comparisons between two apparently dissimilar things. Similes are explicit comparisons using the words *like* or *as,* and metaphors are implicit comparisons. To return to the previous example, if I say, "My boss, Bob, was waiting for me when I showed up to work five minutes late today—the snake!" I have constructed a metaphor. Writing about his experiences fighting in World War I, Wilfred Owen begins his poem "Dulce et decorum est" with a string of similes: "Bent double, like old beggars under sacks, / Knock-kneed, coughing like hags, we cursed through sludge." Owen's goal was to undercut clichéd notions that war and dying in battle were glorious. Certainly, comparing soldiers to coughing hags and to beggars underscores his point.

"Fog," a short poem by Carl Sandburg provides a clear example of a metaphor. Sandburg's poem reads:

The fog comes
on little cat feet.

It sits looking
over harbor and city
on silent haunches
and then moves on.

Notice how effectively Sandburg conveys surprising impressions of the fog by comparing two seemingly disparate things—the fog and a cat.

Symbols, by contrast, are things that stand for, or represent, other things. Often they represent something intangible, such as concepts or ideas. In everyday life we use and understand symbols easily. Babies at christenings and brides at weddings wear white to represent purity. Think, too, of a dollar bill. The paper itself has no value in and of itself. Instead, that paper bill is a symbol of something else, the precious metal in a nation's coffers. Symbols in literature work similarly. Authors use symbols to evoke more than a simple, straightforward, literal meaning. Characters, objects, and places can all function as symbols. Famous literary examples of symbols include Moby-Dick, the white whale of Herman Melville's novel, and the scarlet *A* of Nathaniel Hawthorne's *The Scarlet Letter*. As both of these symbols suggest, a literary symbol cannot be adequately defined or explained by any one meaning. Hester Prynne's Puritan community clearly intends her scarlet *A* as a symbol of her adultery, but as the novel progresses, even her own community reads the letter as representing not just *adultery*, but *able, angel*, and a host of other meanings.

Writing about imagery and symbols requires close attention to the author's language. To prepare a paper on symbolism or imagery in a work, identify and trace the images and symbols and then try to draw some conclusions about how they function. Ask yourself how any symbols or images help contribute to the themes or meanings of the work. What connotations do they carry? How do they affect your reception of the work? Do they shed light on characters or settings? A strong paper on imagery or symbolism will thoroughly consider the use of figures in the text and will try to reach some conclusions about how or why the author uses them.

WRITING ABOUT HISTORY AND CONTEXT

As noted above, it is possible to write an analytical paper that also considers the work's context. After all, the text was not created in a vacuum. The author lived and wrote in a specific time period and in a specific cultural context and, like all of us, was shaped by that environment. Learning more about the historical and cultural circumstances that surround the author and the work can help illuminate a text and provide you with productive material for a paper. Remember, though, that when you write analytical papers, you should use the context to illuminate the text. Do not lose sight of your goal—to interpret the meaning of the literary work. Use historical or philosophical research as a tool to develop your textual evaluation.

Thoughtful readers often consider how history and culture affected the author's choice and treatment of his or her subject matter. Investigations into the history and context of a work could examine the work's relation to specific historical events, such as the Salem witch trials in 17th-century Massachusetts or the restoration of Charles to the British throne in 1660. Bear in mind that historical context is not limited to politics and world events. While knowing about the Vietnam War is certainly helpful in interpreting much of Tim O'Brien's fiction, and some knowledge of the French Revolution clearly illuminates the dynamics of Charles Dickens's *A Tale of Two Cities*, historical context also entails the fabric of daily life. Examining a text in light of gender roles, race relations, class boundaries, or working conditions can give rise to thoughtful and compelling papers. Exploring the conditions of the working class in 19th-century England, for example, can provide a particularly effective avenue for writing about Dickens's *Hard Times*.

You can begin thinking about these issues by asking broad questions at first. What do you know about the time period and about the author? What does the editorial apparatus in your text tell you? These might be starting places. Similarly, when specific historical events or dynamics are particularly important to understanding a work but might be somewhat obscure to modern readers, textbooks usually provide notes to explain historical background. These are a good place to start. With this information, ask yourself how these historical facts and circumstances might have affected the author, the presentation of theme, and the presentation of character. How does knowing more about the work's specific historical context illuminate the work? To take a well-known example, understanding the complex attitudes toward slavery during the time Mark Twain wrote *Adventures of Huckleberry Finn* should help you begin to examine issues of race in the text. Additionally, you might compare these attitudes to those of the time in which the novel was set. How might this comparison affect your interpretation of a work written after the abolition of slavery but set before the Civil War?

WRITING ABOUT PHILOSOPHY AND IDEAS

Philosophical concerns are closely related to both historical context and thematic issues. Like historical investigation, philosophical research can provide a useful tool as you analyze a text. For example, an investigation into the working class in Dickens's England might lead you to a topic on the philosophical doctrine of utilitarianism in *Hard Times.* Many other works explore philosophies and ideas quite explicitly. Mary Shelley's famous novel *Frankenstein,* for example, explores John Locke's tabula rasa theory of human knowledge as she portrays the intellectual and emotional development of Victor Frankenstein's creature. As this example indicates, philosophical issues are somewhat more abstract than investigations of theme or historical context. Some other examples of philosophical issues include human free will, the formation of human identity, the nature of sin, or questions of ethics.

Writing about philosophy and ideas might require some outside research, but usually the notes or other material in your text will provide you with basic information and often footnotes and bibliographies suggest places you can go to read further about the subject. If you have identified a philosophical theme that runs through a text, you might ask yourself how the author develops this theme. Look at character development and the interactions of characters, for example. Similarly, you might examine whether the narrative voice in a work of fiction addresses the philosophical concerns of the text.

WRITING COMPARE AND CONTRAST ESSAYS

Finally, you might find that comparing and contrasting the works or techniques of an author provides a useful tool for literary analysis. A comparison and contrast essay might compare two characters or themes in a single work, or it might compare the author's treatment of a theme in two works. It might also contrast methods of character development or analyze an author's differing treatment of a philosophical concern in two works. Writing comparison and contrast essays, though, requires some special consideration. While they generally provide you with plenty of material to use, they also come with a built-in trap: the laundry list. These papers often become mere lists of connections between the works. As this chapter will discuss, a strong thesis must make an assertion that you want to prove or validate. A strong comparison/contrast thesis, then, needs to comment on the significance of the similarities and differences you observe. It is not enough merely to assert that the works contain similarities and differences. You might, for example, assert why the similarities and differences are important and explain how they illuminate the works' treatment of theme. Remember, too, that a thesis should not be a statement of the obvious. A comparison/contrast paper that focuses only on very obvious similarities or differences does little to illuminate the connections between the works. Often, an effective method of shaping a strong thesis and argument is to begin your paper by noting the similarities between the works but then to develop a thesis that asserts how these apparently similar elements are different. If, for example, you observe that Emily Dickinson wrote a number of poems about spiders, you might analyze how she uses spider imagery differently in two poems. Similarly, many scholars have noted that Hawthorne created many "mad scientist" characters, men who are so devoted to their science or their art that they lose perspective on all else. A good thesis comparing two of these characters—Aylmer of "The Birthmark" and Dr. Rappaccini of "Rappaccini's Daughter," for example—might initially identify both characters as examples of Hawthorne's mad scientist type but then argue that their motivations for scientific experimentation differ. If you strive to analyze the similarities or differences, discuss significances, and move beyond the obvious, your paper should move beyond the laundry list trap.

PREPARING TO WRITE

Armed with a clear sense of your task—illuminating the text—and with an understanding of theme, character, language, history, and philosophy, you are ready to approach the writing process. Remember that good writing is grounded in good reading and that close reading takes time, attention, and more than one reading of your text. Read for comprehension first. As you go back and review the work, mark the text to chart the details of the work as well as your reactions. Highlight important passages, repeated words, and image patterns. "Converse" with the text through marginal notes. Mark turns in the plot, ask questions, and make observations about characters, themes, and language. If you are reading from a book that does not belong to you, keep a record of your reactions in a journal or notebook. If you have read a work of literature carefully, paying attention to both the text and the context of the work, you have a leg up on the writing process. Admittedly, at this point, your ideas are probably very broad and undefined, but you have taken an important first step toward writing a strong paper.

Your next step is to focus, to take a broad, perhaps fuzzy, topic and define it more clearly. Even a topic provided by your instructor will need to be focused appropriately. Remember that good writers make the topic their own. There are a number of strategies—often called "invention"— that you can use to develop your own focus. In one such strategy, *freewriting*, you spend 10 minutes or so just writing about your topic without referring back to the text or your notes. Write whatever comes to mind; the important thing is that you just keep writing. Often this process allows you to develop fresh ideas or approaches to your subject matter. You could also try *brainstorming*. Write down your topic and then list all the related points or ideas you can think of. Include questions, comments, words, important passages or events, and anything else that comes to mind. Let one idea lead to another. In the related technique of *clustering*, or *mapping*, write your topic on a sheet of paper and write related ideas around it. Then list related sub points under each of these main ideas. Many people then draw arrows to show connections between points. This technique helps you narrow your topic and can also help you organize your ideas. Similarly, asking journalistic questions—Who? What? Where? When? Why? and How?—can develop ideas for topic development.

Thesis Statements

Once you have developed a focused topic, you can begin to think about your thesis statement, the main point or purpose of your paper. It is absolutely imperative that you craft a strong thesis; otherwise, your paper will likely be little more than random, disorganized observations about the text. Think of your thesis statement as a kind of road map of your paper. It tells readers where you are going and how you are going to get there.

In order to craft a good thesis, you must keep a number of things in mind. First, as the title of this subsection indicates, your paper's thesis should be a statement, an assertion about the text that you want to prove or validate. Often, beginning writers formulate a question that they attempt to use as a thesis. For example, a writer exploring the friendship between Sula Peace and Nel Wright in Morrison's *Sula* might ask, How are Sula and Nel connected? While such a question is a good strategy to use in the invention process to help narrow your topic and find your thesis, it cannot serve as the thesis statement, because it does not tell your reader what you want to assert about the two characters. A writer might shape this question into a thesis by instead proposing an answer to that question: After the experience with Chicken Little's death, Sula and Nel develop a friendship that requires no words. Even after Nel feels betrayed by Sula, she realizes that they will always be connected. Notice that this thesis provides an initial plan or structure for the rest of the paper, and notice too that the thesis statement does not necessarily have to fit into one sentence. After establishing the relationship they develop, the writer could examine the ways in which Sula is presented as being unaware of her betrayal of Nel and then continue to show how even over time, the two friends need each other more than they think.

Second, remember that a good thesis makes an assertion that you need to support. In other words, a good thesis does not state the obvious. If you tried to formulate a thesis about *Sula* by saying, Morrison's Sula is a woman who returns to her community, you've done nothing but rephrase the obvious. Since Morrison describes Sula's return in detail, there would be no point in spending three to five pages to support that assertion. You might try to develop a thesis by asking yourself some further questions about that point: What does it mean to return to one's community after a long absence? Does the story seem to indicate that returning to your roots is a positive thing? Does it praise Sula for remaining on the periphery of her community or does it criticize her because of it? Such a line of questioning might lead you to a more viable thesis, like the one in the preceding paragraph.

As the comparison with the road map also suggests, your thesis should appear near the beginning of the paper. In relatively short papers (three to six pages), the thesis almost always appears in the first paragraph. Some writers fall into the trap of saving their thesis for the end, trying to provide a surprise or a big moment of revelation. (As if to say, "I've just proven that Morrison uses the character of Cholly Breedlove in *The Bluest Eye* to reflect a reality that damaged people can destroy their own family members through their actions.") Placing a thesis at the end of an essay can seriously mar the essay's effectiveness. If you fail to clearly define your essay's point and purpose at the beginning, it makes it difficult for your reader to assess the clarity of your argument and understand the points you are making. Your argument should not come as a surprise to the reader at the end. When you do this, you have forced your reader to reread your essay in order to assess its logic and effectiveness.

Finally, you should avoid using the first person ("I") as you present your thesis. Though it is not strictly wrong to write in the first person, it is difficult to do so gracefully. While writing in the first person, beginning writers often fall into the trap of writing self-reflexive prose (writing *about* their paper *in* their paper). Often this leads to the most dreaded of opening lines: "In this paper I am going to discuss. . . ." Not only does this self-reflexive voice make for very awkward prose, it frequently allows writers to boldly announce a topic while completely avoiding a thesis statement. An example might be a paper that begins: `Beloved, Morrison's most famous novel, follows the life of Sethe, who has committed infanticide and is forced to suffer the consequences of her actions. In this paper I am going to discuss the significance of the infanticide in the novel.` The author of this paper has done little more than announce a topic for the paper (the significance of the infanticide). While she may have intended the last sentence as a thesis, she fails to present her opinion about the significance of infanticide. To improve this "thesis" the writer would need to back up a couple of steps. First, the announced topic of the paper is too broad; infanticide has to be put into the social and historical context of slavery. The writer should first consider some of the many functions of the act of infanticide within Morrison's text.

From here, the author could select the function that seems most appealing, and then begin to craft a specific thesis. A writer who chooses to explore Sethe's act might, for example, craft a thesis that reads, Sethe challenges the worldview of slave masters by killing her child and thus preventing her from living the life of a slave. Her act has many repercussions that affect herself, Beloved, and Denver.

Outlines

While developing a strong, thoughtful thesis early in your writing process should help focus your paper, outlining provides an essential tool for logically shaping that paper. A good outline helps you see—and develop—the relationships between the points in your argument and assures you that your paper flows logically and coherently. Outlining not only helps to place your points in a logical order, it also helps you subordinate supporting points, weed out any irrelevant points, and decide if there are any necessary points that are missing from your argument. Most of us are familiar with formal outlines that use numerical and letter designations for each point. Remember, though, that there are different types of outlines; you may find that an informal outline is a more useful tool for you. What is important, though, is that you spend the time to develop some sort of outline—formal or informal.

Remember that an outline is a tool to help you shape and write a strong paper. If you do not spend sufficient time planning your supporting points and shaping the arrangement of those points, you will most likely construct a vague, unfocused outline that provides little, if any, help with the writing of the paper. Consider the following example:

Thesis: Sethe challenges the worldview of slave masters by killing her child and thus preventing her from living the life of a slave. Her act has many repercussions that affect herself, Beloved, and Denver.

    I. Introduction and thesis

   II. Sethe
      A. Her chokecherry tree

       B. Amy Denver's role in her escape from
         Sweet Home
       C. Her murder of the baby

   III. Beloved

    IV. Slave masters
       A. Their worldview

     V. Paul D

    VI. Conclusion
       A. Sethe challenges slave masters' world-
         view

This outline has a number of flaws. First of all, the major topics labeled with the Roman numerals are not arranged in a logical order. If the paper's aim is to show how Sethe functions as a challenge to slave master attitudes, the writer should define those attitudes before presenting Sethe as a challenge to them. Similarly, the thesis makes no reference to Paul D, but the writer includes him as a major section of this outline. As someone who helps Sethe figure out many details about her past, he may well have a place in this paper, but the writer fails to provide detail about his importance to the argument. Third, the writer includes Amy Denver's role in Sethe's escape as one of the lettered items in section II. Letters A and C refer to ways Sethe experiences slave master society and challenges it; Amy Denver's role does not belong in this list. One could argue that Amy Denver's help, like Sethe, is a challenge to slave master attitudes, but unlike the other items, it is not one of Sethe's challenges. A fourth problem is the inclusion of a letter *A* in Sections IV and VI. An outline should not include an *A* without a *B*, a *1* without a *2*, etc. The final problem with this outline is the overall lack of detail. None of the sections provide much information about the content of the argument, and it seems likely that the writer has not given sufficient thought to the content of the paper. A better start to this outline might be:

Thesis: Sethe challenges the worldview of slave masters by killing her child and thus preventing her from living the life of a slave. Her act has many repercussions that affect herself, Beloved, and Denver.

I. Introduction and thesis

II. The slave master worldview
   A. Slave master attitudes
   B. Treatment of slaves at Sweet Home

III. Sethe's challenges to slave master attitudes
   A. Escape
   B. Infanticide

IV. Effect on Denver
   A. Inability to connect to others
   B. Isolation from the community

V. Effect on Beloved
   A. Haunts the house
   B. Returns to seek revenge

VI. Conclusion
   A. Sethe escapes successfully and challenges the system
   B. Her challenge to the system of slavery literally and figuratively haunts her

This new outline, then, would prove much more helpful when it came time to write the paper.

An outline like this could be shaped into an even more useful tool if the writer fleshed out the argument by providing specific examples from the text to support each point. Once you have listed your main point and the supporting ideas, develop this raw material by listing related supporting ideas and material under each of those main headings. From there, arrange the material in subsections and order the material logically. For example, you might begin with one of the theses cited above, After the experience with Chicken Little's death, Sula and Nel develop a friendship that requires no words. Even after Nel feels betrayed by Sula, she realizes that they will always be connected. As noted above, this thesis already gives you the beginning of an organization: Start by supporting the notion that Chicken Little's death creates an unspoken bond, and then explain how Morrison casts their relationship as indestructible. You might start your outline, then, with three topic headings: 1) The impact of Chicken Little's death; 2) Sula's betrayal of Nel; 3) their lasting friendship. Under each of those headings you could then list ideas that support that particular point. Be sure to include references to parts of the text that help build your case. An informal outline, then, might look like this:

Thesis: After the experience with Chicken Little's death, Sula and Nel develop a friendship that requires no words. Even after Nel feels betrayed by Sula, she realizes that they will always be connected.

1. Chicken Little's death
   - The accident of Chicken Little's drowning
     - All three are children
     - Sula and Nel become accomplices in an act that no one else witnesses
   - Effects of his death
     - Sula feels responsible
     - Nel goes on to experience the pressure of perfection from her mother

2. Sula's betrayal of Nel
   - Sula's sexual relationship with Jude
     - Her attitude is one of nonchalance
     - Sula does not feel she is crossing a moral boundary
   - Nel's reaction:
     - She feels betrayed

○ She feels the community is right in their mistrust and ostracism of Sula

  3. Their lasting friendship
- The irony of their friendship:
  - ○ Nel's conformity to societal rules
  - ○ Sula's behavior connects her to the legacy of Peace women who reject society's rules
- Sula is left alone without help from the community
  - ○ Nel visits and tries to help Sula
  - ○ Sula admonishes Nel for not forgiving her for the act
  - ○ Sula dies alone

Conclusion:
- Nel feels a sense of loss and realizes her love for Sula

You would set about writing a formal outline with a similar process, though in the final stages you would label the headings differently. A formal outline for a paper that argues the thesis cited about *The Bluest Eye*—that Morrison uses the character Cholly Breedlove in the story to reflect a reality that humans are neither evil nor pure, but a mixture of both—might look like this:

Thesis: Morrison uses the character of Cholly Breedlove in *The Bluest Eye* to reflect a reality that damaged people can destroy their own family members through their "private" actions.

    I. Introduction and thesis

    II. Morrison's statement that the book was a public airing of private matters
       A. Incest as a private matter

B. The child narrator who airs this private
        matter
          1. Irony of a child telling this story
          2. The ways children are mistreated in
            the novel

III. Cholly's character
      A. We see him in contrast to the Dick and
        Jane family
          1. Metaphorical and literal meanings of
            Dick and Jane story
          2. How he is the antithesis of the Dick
            and Jane story
      B. He is portrayed as a monster at first
          1. Initial descriptions of his drunken-
            ness from Pauline's perspective
          2. Stereotypical associations of black
            men

IV. Cholly's history
      A. We get the story of his past
      B. His abandonment and search for his father
      C. His rebirth and slide into alcoholism

V. Conclusion
      A. How Cholly's actions have far-reaching
        effects on Pecola Breedlove at the end
        of the story
      B. The ways the destruction affects family
        members and others in the community.

As with the previous example, the thesis provided the seeds of a structure, and the writer was careful to arrange the supporting points in a logical manner, showing the relationships between the ideas in the paper.

Body Paragraphs

Once your outline is complete, you can begin drafting your paper. Paragraphs, units of related sentences, are the building blocks of a good paper, and as you draft you should keep in mind both the function and the qualities of good paragraphs. Paragraphs help you chart and control the shape and content of your essay, and they help the reader to see your organization and your logic. You should begin a new paragraph whenever you move from one major point to another. In longer, more complex essays you might use a group of related paragraphs to help support major points. Remember that in addition to being adequately developed, a good paragraph is both unified and coherent.

Unified Paragraphs

Each paragraph must be centralized around one idea or point, and a unified paragraph carefully focuses on and develops this central idea without including extraneous ideas or tangents. For beginning writers, the best way to be assured that you are constructing unified paragraphs is to include a topic sentence in each paragraph. This topic sentence should convey the main point of the paragraph, and every sentence in the paragraph should relate back to that topic sentence. Any sentence that strays from the central topic does not belong in the paragraph and needs to be revised or deleted. Consider the following paragraph about Sula's nonconformity. Notice how the paragraph veers away from the main point that Sula rejects the societal norms that Medallion sets up:

> Sula returns to the Bottom and sets about breaking every single taboo in the community. This idea of nonconformity is central to the plot, and creates a great deal of conflict that Sula struggles with internally. Sula soon falls in love with Ajax, and he surprises her with unusual gifts, such as filling the room with butterflies. She later finds out that he is really called Albert Jacks. All along she thought she knew who he was, but she finds out that even she could be fooled by someone. She feels betrayed and gives up on love.

While the paragraph begins solidly, and the second sentence provides the central theme, the author soon goes on a tangent. If the purpose of the paragraph is to demonstrate that Sula is a nonconformist, the sentences about Ajax's eventual betrayal of her are tangential here. They may find a place later in the paper, but they should be deleted from this paragraph.

Coherent Paragraphs

In addition to shaping unified paragraphs, you must also craft coherent paragraphs, paragraphs that develop their points logically with sentences that flow smoothly into one another. Coherence depends on the order of your sentences, but it is not strictly the order of the sentences that is important to paragraph coherence. You also need to craft your prose to help the reader see the relationship between the sentences. Consider the following paragraph about Sula's nonconformity. Notice how the writer uses the same ideas as the paragraph above but fails to help the reader see the relationships between the points:

> Sula returns to the Bottom and sets about breaking every single taboo in the community. This idea of nonconformity is central to the plot, and creates a great deal of conflict that Sula struggles with internally. Sula's nonconformity is interesting when she says at the end of the novel, "I sure did live in this world" (145). Nel never gets a chance to be a nonconformist because she grew up with her mother's insistence on perfection and trying to please others in the community. Sula also tells Nel, "I don't know everything, I just do everything" (143).

This paragraph demonstrates that unity alone does not guarantee paragraph effectiveness. The argument is hard to follow because the author fails both to show connections between the sentences and to indicate how they work to support the overall point.

A number of techniques are available to aid paragraph coherence. Careful use of transitional words and phrases is essential. You can use transitional flags to introduce an example or an illustration (*for example, for instance*); to amplify a point or add another phase of the same idea (*additionally, furthermore, next, similarly, finally, then*); to indicate a conclusion or result (*therefore, as a result, thus, in other words*); to signal a contrast or a qualification (*on the other hand, nevertheless, despite this, on the contrary, still, however, conversely*); to signal a comparison (*likewise, in comparison, similarly*); and to indicate a movement in time (*afterward, earlier, eventually, finally, later, subsequently, until*).

In addition to transitional flags, careful use of pronouns aids coherence and flow. If you were writing about *The Wizard of Oz*, you would not want to keep repeating, the phrase "the witch" or the name "Dorothy." Careful substitution of the pronoun "she" in these instances can aid coherence. A word of warning, though: When you substitute pronouns for proper names, always be sure that your pronoun reference is clear. In a paragraph that discusses both Dorothy and the witch, substituting "she" could lead to confusion. Make sure that it is clear to whom the pronoun refers. Generally, the pronoun refers to the last proper noun you have used.

While repeating the same name over and over again can lead to awkward, boring prose, it is possible to use repetition to help your paragraph's coherence. Careful repetition of important words or phrases can lend coherence to your paragraph by helping remind readers of your key points. Admittedly, it takes some practice to use this technique effectively. You may find that reading your prose aloud can help you develop an ear for effective use of repetition.

To see how helpful transitional aids are, compare the paragraph below to the previous example about Sula's nonconformity. Notice how the author works with the same ideas and quotations but shapes them into a much more coherent paragraph whose point is clearer and easier to follow:

```
Sula returns to the Bottom and sets about breaking
every single taboo in the community. This idea of
nonconformity is central to the plot, and creates a great
deal of conflict that Sula struggles with internally.
Sula's nonconformity is interesting when contrasted to
Nel's sense of responsibility to do what her mother
taught her in order to fit into the community. Nel never
gets a chance to be a nonconformist because she grew up
with her mother's insistence on perfection and trying
to please others in the community. Sula's rejection of
rules clashes with Nel's conformity, as is evidenced
when Sula tells Nel, "I don't know everything, I just do
```

everything" (143). An example of her rejecting society's constraints is when she says at the end of the novel, "I sure did live in this world" (145), as opposed to Nel, who lives a life that is restrained.

Introductions

Introductions and conclusions present particular challenges for writers. Generally, your introduction should do two things: capture your reader's attention and explain the main point of your essay. In other words, while your introduction should contain your thesis, it needs to do a bit more work than that. You are likely to find that starting that first paragraph is one of the most difficult parts of the paper. It is hard to face that blank page or screen, and as a result, many beginning writers, in desperation to start somewhere, start with overly broad, general statements. While it is often a good strategy to start with more general subject matter and narrow your focus, do not begin with broad sweeping statements like, "Names are important to everyone," or "Throughout the history of literature, many authors have used names to express their points." Such sentences are nothing but empty filler. They begin to fill the blank page, but they do nothing to advance your argument. Instead, you might try to gain your readers' interest. Some writers like to begin with a pertinent quotation or with a relevant question. Or, you might begin with an introduction of the topic you will discuss. If you are writing about Morrison's use of names in *Sula*, for instance, you might begin by talking about the importance of naming in African-American culture. Another common trap to avoid is depending on your title to introduce the author and the text you are writing about. Always include the work's author and title in your opening paragraph.

Compare the effectiveness of the following introductions:

1. Throughout history, names have had significance. For example, think about the names Joy, Love, and Peace. In this novel, Morrison uses names to reflect African-American society.

2. In many cultures, particular names carry specific meanings. African-American culture is

> no exception. Since names have been used to
> reinforce African-American people's inferior
> status in society, renaming a person takes on
> political and social significance. Often writers
> incorporate these naming strategies into their
> works to reinforce their meanings. In *Sula*,
> Toni Morrison uses naming to reflect the unique
> character traits of various individuals.

The first introduction begins with a boring, overly broad sentence, cites unclear, undeveloped examples, and then moves abruptly to the thesis. Notice, too, how a reader deprived of the paper's title does not know the title of the story that the paper will analyze. The second introduction works with the same material and thesis, but provides more detail, and is, consequently, much more interesting. It begins by discussing cultural uses of names, gives specific examples, and then speaks briefly about the use of naming in literature. The paragraph ends with the thesis, which includes both the author and the title of the work to be discussed.

The paragraph below provides another example of an opening strategy. It begins by introducing the author and the text it will analyze, and then it moves on to briefly introduce relevant details of the novel in order to set up its thesis:

> In *The Bluest Eye*, Toni Morrison first introduces Cholly
> Breedlove as one who has created a difficult reality
> for his family to live with. The definition of his
> name would suggest his propensity for creating love.
> The reader soon finds out that his name is ironic,
> and that actually he has only created fear and misery
> in his family through his despicable actions. Cholly's
> actions are representative of what Morrison calls the
> "the public exposure of a private confidence" (212). The
> reader experiences the exposure of Cholly's actions. We
> also see his background and the anger and disappointment
> that framed his life and may have turned him into an
> abuser.

Conclusions

Conclusions present another series of challenges for writers. No doubt you have heard the old adage about writing papers: "Tell us what you are going to say, say it, and then tell us what you've said." While this formula does not necessarily result in bad papers, it does not necessarily result in good ones either. It will almost certainly result in boring papers (especially boring conclusions). If you have done a good job establishing your points in the body of the paper, the reader already knows and understands your argument. There is no need to merely reiterate. Do not just summarize your main points in your conclusion. Such a boring and mechanical conclusion does nothing to advance your argument or interest your reader. Consider the following conclusion to the paper about naming in *Sula*:

> In conclusion, Morrison uses names to tell her reader a lot about humanity. Sula Peace lives a life that is not so peaceful. Nel Wright finds out she is not always right.

Besides starting with a mechanical and obvious transitional device, this conclusion does little more than summarize the main points of the outline (and it does not even touch on all of them). It is incomplete and uninteresting.

Instead, your conclusion should add something to your paper. A good tactic is to build upon the points you have been arguing. Asking "why?" often helps to draw further conclusions. For example, in the paper discussed above, you might speculate or explain why naming is effective in *Sula*. You could approach the novel's focus on African-American life, and examine the ways Morrison bestows her characters with complexity at a time when African Americans were not portrayed as multidimensional. Another method of successfully concluding a paper is to speculate on other directions in which to take your topic, tie it into larger issues. It might help to envision your paper as just one section of a larger paper. Having established your points in this paper, how would you build upon this argument? Where would you go next? In the following conclusion to the paper on *Sula*, the author reiterates some of the main points of the paper, but does so in order to amplify the discussion of the story's sociological message:

In the end, Morrison's characters are complex, and this complexity emerges through the characterization of African Americans, who were historically misrepresented. The names of the various characters often relate to their behavior, and the humor contained in the names allows the reader to experience levity interspersed with grave situations and events.

Citations and Formatting

Using Primary Sources

As the examples included in this chapter indicate, strong papers on literary texts incorporate quotations from the text in order to support their points. It is not enough for you to assert your interpretation without providing support or evidence from the text. Without well-chosen quotations to support your argument you are, in effect, just saying to the reader, "Take my word for it." It is important to use quotations thoughtfully and selectively. Remember that the paper presents *your* argument, so choose quotations that support *your* assertions. Do not let the author's voice overwhelm your own. With that caution in mind, there are some guidelines you should follow to ensure that you use quotations clearly and effectively.

Integrate Quotations

Quotations should always be integrated into your own prose. Do not just drop them into your paper without introduction or comment. Otherwise, it is unlikely that your reader will see their function. You can integrate textual support easily and clearly with identifying tags, short phrases that identify the speaker. For example:

The narrator describes Sula's attitude toward men by saying, "With the exception of BoyBoy, those Peace women loved all men (25)."

While this tag appears before the quotation, you can also use tags after or in the middle of the quoted text. For example:

"Shadrack rose and returned to the cot, where he fell into the first sleep of his new life," bringing to an end his earlier torment (13-14).

You can also use a colon to formally introduce a quotation:

```
Sula's message is clear: "Yes. But my lonely is mine"
(143).
```

Longer quotations (more than four lines of prose) should be set off from the rest of your paper in a block quotation. Double space before you begin the passage, indent it ten spaces from your left-hand margin, and double space the passage itself. Because the indentation signals the inclusion of a quotation, do not use quotation marks around the cited passage. Use a colon to introduce the passage:

```
Nel soon realizes the repercussions of Sula's act of
betrayal:

    The clock was ticking. Nel looked at it. And
    realized that it was two-thirty, only forty-five
    minutes before the children would be home and
    she hadn't even felt anything right or sensible
    and now there was no time or wouldn't be until
    nighttime when they were asleep and she could
    get into bed and maybe she could do it then.
    Think. But who could think in that bed where
    they had been and where they also had been and
    where only she was now? (106–107)

By now, the reader should realize that Nel and Sula's
relationship has been irreparably damaged.
```

It is also important to interpret quotations after you introduce them. Explain how they help to advance your point. You cannot assume that your reader would interpret the quotations the same way that you do.

Quote Accurately

Always quote accurately. Anything within quotations marks must be the author's *exact* words. There are, however, some rules to follow if you need to modify the quotation to fit into your prose.

a) Use brackets to indicate any material that might have been added to the author's exact wording. For example, if you need to add any words to the quotation or alter it grammatically to allow it to fit into your prose, indicate your changes in brackets:

> "Nel blinked but acquiesced. [Nel and Sula] walked up the street until they got to the bend of Carpenter's Road where the boys lounged on a disused well" (54).

b) Conversely, if you choose to omit any words from the quotation, use ellipses (three spaced periods) to indicate missing words or phrases:

> Nel feels "This very grief . . . would be gone" (108).

c) If you delete a sentence or more, use the ellipses after a period:

> The narrator indicates, "But that was the terrible part, the effort it took not to look. . . . It was so nice to think about their scary dreams and not a ball of fur" (109).

Punctuate Properly

Punctuation of quotations often causes more trouble than it should. Once again, you just need to keep these simple rules in mind.

a) The period or comma goes after the citation (more on these later in this chapter):

> Sula's message to Nel is clear: "Yes. But my lonely is *mine*" (143).

b) Other marks of punctuation—colons, semicolons, question marks, and exclamation points—go outside the quotation marks unless they are part of the original quotation:

> Why does the narrator say that "Nel and Sula did
> not touch hands or look at each other during
> the funeral" (64)?
>
> Nel wonders, "Was there anyone else before whom
> she could never be foolish?" (95).

Documenting Primary Sources

Unless you are instructed otherwise, you should provide sufficient information for your reader to locate material you quote. Generally, literature papers follow the rules set forth by the Modern Language Association. These can be found in the *MLA Handbook for Writers of Research Papers* (sixth edition). You should be able to find this book in the reference section of your library. Additionally, its rules for citing both primary and secondary sources are widely available from reputable online sources. One source is the Online Writing Lab [OWL] at Purdue University. OWL's guide to MLA style is available at http://owl. english.purdue.edu/owl/resource/557/01/. The Modern Language Association also includes answers to frequently asked questions about MLA style on this helpful web page: http://www.mla.org/style_faq. Generally, when you are citing from literary works in papers, you should keep a few guidelines in mind.

Parenthetical Citations

MLA asks for parenthetical references in your text after quotations. When you are working with prose (short stories, novels, or essays) include page numbers in the parentheses:

> Sula's message to Nel is clear: "Yes. But my lonely is
> *mine*" (143).

The Works Cited Page

These parenthetical citations are then linked to a separate works cited page at the end of the paper. The works cited page lists works alphabetically by the authors' last names. An entry for the above reference to Morrison's *Sula* would read:

```
Morrison, Toni. Sula. New York: Knopf, 1973.
```

The *MLA Handbook* includes a full listing of sample entries, as do many of the online explanations of MLA style.

Documenting Secondary Sources

In order to assure that your paper is built entirely upon your own ideas and analysis, instructors often ask that you write interpretative papers without any outside research. If, on the other hand, your paper requires research, you must document any secondary sources you use. You need to document direct quotations, summaries, or paraphrases of other's ideas and factual information that is not common knowledge. Follow the guidelines above for quoting primary sources when you use direct quotations from secondary sources. Keep in mind that MLA style also includes very specific guidelines for citing electronic sources. OWL's website provides a nice summary: http://owl.english.purdue.edu/owl/resource/557/09/.

Parenthetical Citations

As with the documentation of primary sources described above, MLA guidelines require in-text parenthetical references to your secondary sources. Unlike the research papers you might write for a history class, literary research papers following MLA style do not use footnotes as a means of documenting sources. Instead, after a quotation, you should cite the author's last name and the page number:

> "Just as important as the principle of humanism, Milkman must learn egalitarianism, the inherent equality of every human being" (Mbalia 62).

If you include the name of the author in your prose, then you would include only the page number in your citation. For example:

> According to Doreatha Drummond Mbalia, "Just as important as the principle of humanism, Milkman must learn egalitarianism, the inherent quality of every human being" (62).

If you are including more than one work by the same author, the parenthetical citation should include an identifiable word or words from the title in order to indicate which of the author's works you cite. For example:

> Morrison writes that "[T]he presence of evil was something to be first recognized, then dealt with, survived, outwitted, triumphed over" (*Sula* 118).

Similarly, if you summarize the particular ideas of your source, you must provide documentation:

> Milkman's journey brings him to an understanding of the fact that people are equals in society (Mbalia 62).

The Works Cited Page

As with the primary sources discussed above, the parenthetical references are keyed to a separate works cited page at the end of the paper. Here is an example of a works cited page that uses the examples cited above. You can find a complete list of sample entries in the *MLA Handbook* or from a reputable online summary of MLA style.

WORKS CITED

Mbalia, Doreatha Drummond. *Toni Morrison's Developing Class Consciousness.* 2d ed. Selinsgrove, PA: Susquehanna UP, 2004.

Morrison, Toni. *Sula.* New York: Knopf, 1973.

——. *The Bluest Eye.* New York: Holt, Rinehart and Winston, 1970.

Plagiarism

Failure to document carefully and thoroughly can leave you open to charges of stealing the ideas of others, which is known as plagiarism, and this is a very serious matter. Remember that it is important to use quotation marks when you use distinct language used by your source, even if you use just one or two words. For example, if you wrote, Milkman must learn egalitarianism, you would be guilty of plagiarism, since you used Mbalia's distinct language without acknowledging her as the source. Instead, you should write: Milkman's journey enables him to "learn egalitarianism" (Mbalia 62). In this case, you have properly credited Mbalia.

Similarly, neither summarizing the ideas of an author nor changing or omitting just a few words means that you can omit a citation. Doreatha Drummond Mbalia's book on Morrison's work contains the following passage about the novel *Song of Solomon*:

> Significantly, it is not until after Milkman has revolutionized his consciousness in regard to race oppression and class exploitation that he sheds his sexist views of women. Prior to this increased awareness, Milkman, as his name suggests, milks the life out of women, giving them nothing in return. As pointed out, so reactionary is his view of women that he has difficulty distinguishing his mother from his sisters and rarely thinks of any of them.

Below are two examples of plagiarized passages:

> Milkman's chauvinism causes him to take everything he can from women, without reciprocating.

> Milkman goes through a profound change in the novel and gives up his chauvinistic ways of seeing women. Before his change, he milks the life out of women, giving them nothing in return (Mbalia 63).

While the first passage doesn't use Mbalia's exact language, it does present the same people she connects to Milkman without citing her work. Since this view is her distinct idea, this constitutes plagiarism. The second passage has shortened her passage, changed some wording, and included a citation, but some of the phrasing is Mbalia's. The first passage could be fixed with a parenthetical citation. Because some of the wording remains the same, though, the second would require the use of quotation marks in addition to a parenthetical citation. The passage below represents an honestly and adequately documented use of the original passage:

> Milkman "sheds his sexist views of women," according to Doreatha Mbalia. "Prior to this increased awareness, Milkman, as his name suggests, milks the life out of women, giving them nothing in return" (62).

This passage acknowledges that this idea is derived from Mbalia while appropriately using quotations to indicate her precise language.

While it is not necessary to document well-known facts, often referred to as "common knowledge," any ideas or language that you take from someone else must be properly documented. Common knowledge generally includes the birth and death dates of authors or other well-documented facts of their lives. An often-cited guideline is: If you can find the information in three sources, it is common knowledge. Despite this guideline, it is, admittedly, often difficult to know if the facts you uncover are common knowledge or not. When in doubt, document your source.

Sample Essay

Shajena Erazo
Ms. S. Harrison
English 260
December 1st 2006

Castaway: Implications of Scapegoating through the Character of Pecola Breedlove in Toni Morrison's *The Bluest Eye*

There is a cowardly propensity in the human heart that delights in oppressing somebody else, and in the gratification of this base desire we always select a victim that can be outraged with safety.

—James T. Rapier

It has been said that both literature and life often mimic each other, and the ideas of victimization and scapegoating relate to both. The words spoken by James T. Rapier echo true since it is often human nature to be attracted to those who can be manipulated. Rather than dealing with their own issues, the people of the dominant group govern individuals simply because it can be done and transfer their inadequacies onto those who are often naive and helpless. In Toni Morrison's *The Bluest Eye*, an 11-year-old girl, Pecola Breedlove, becomes the archetypal transference figure for her community, since she embodies the characteristics of a scapegoat and manifests the ugliness that her community fatefully projects on her. While there are varying degrees of scapegoating throughout this text, Pecola Breedlove serves different functions of the scapegoat in her community and suffers psychological trauma as a result.

While scapegoating can be seen as a universal human tendency, the Judeo-Christian framework for understanding the origin of scapegoating has a very interesting history. On the Day of Atonement, better known as Yom Kippur, the high priest would bring in two goats into the Temple in Jerusalem, and "[t]he goat will carry on itself their sins to a solitary place; and the man shall release in the desert" (NIV Lev. 16:22). The term "scapegoat" came from this religious ceremony, and now has literally come to mean "someone selected to bear blame for a calamity." In the same way that the biblical text discusses the transference of sins onto an innocent creature, Pecola Breedlove ultimately becomes the object of her community's hatred and sins, which eventually drive her into insanity and an isolated place outside the borders of the town in which she grew up.

The Breedlove family as a unit can be seen as a scapegoat for their entire community. In describing

the attributes of this family, the text states, "[y]ou looked at them and wondered why they were so ugly . . . you realized that it came from conviction, their conviction . . . they took the ugliness in their hands, threw it as a mantle over them, and went about the world with it" (Morrison 39). This description of the Breedlove family immediately establishes the fact that they are not attractive and worse yet, everyone knows it. While the Breedlove family becomes collectively seen as the scapegoats for their community, since they are outcasts, Pecola becomes the scapegoat for the other black characters in the text, including her family, but in varying degrees. The type of burdens that Pecola carries and the scapegoat that she becomes depends on the other person's role in society and their relation to Pecola. While it may seem easier to simply state that Pecola is a receptacle into which each person "dumped" (205) their failures, inadequacies, and insecurities, it is not sufficient. She is more than just the dumping ground of their fears and unworthiness; she is the absorber of pain and she internalizes that ugliness to construct her own image—an image, unfortunately, that only further encourages the characters to blame her for their inadequacies.

One intriguing example of scapegoating in the text occurs when Claudia, Frieda, and Pecola walk home with Maureen Peal. A group of boys along their path begin to tease Pecola by calling her "Black e mo" and mocking her father by saying, "Ya daddy sleeps nekked" (65). When they taunt her because of her skin color and the fact that her father sleeps naked, both of which Pecola has no control over, transference of insecurities occurs. Pecola now becomes the object whom her peers find ugly. In the same way that the Jewish High Priest used to transmit the sins from the people of Israel unto the goat that was cast out into the wilderness, the boys and Maureen Peal redirect their own insecurities and strengthen their own perception of themselves merely by amplifying the ugliness of Pecola.

The boys are mesmerized by Maureen Peal's light skin, and rather than feeling bad themselves about their darker complexions, they instead relocate their own insecurities and self-hate to Pecola, who is already considered ugly by the people in her town:

> They seemed to have taken all of their smoothly cultivated ignorance, their exquisitely learned self-hatred, their elaborately designed hopelessness and sucked it all up into a fiery cone of scorn that had burned for ages in the hollows of their minds—cooled—and spilled over lips of outrage, consuming whatever was in its path (65).

Morrison describes their "scorn" as if it is a physical brand with which the children disfigure Pecola. Maybe her blackness is a reminder of their blackness. Their decision to have "danced a macabre ballet around the victim, whom, for their own sake, they were prepared to sacrifice to the flaming pit" (65) further depicts the extent to which they are willing to go in order to feel superior to her. Pecola can be seen as a sacrifice, but not in the traditional sense of being a physical sacrifice. Rather, Pecola is the sacrifice because her community projects and externalizes its own fears unto her, until she ultimately internalizes that ugliness only later to be ostracized by the same people who gave it to her.

To further discuss the idea of scapegoats and sacrifice, it is also necessary to see the evolution of these ideas in the Bible. In the book of Isaiah it says: "But he was pierced for our transgressions, he was crushed for our iniquities, the punishment that brought us peace was upon him, and by his wounds we are healed" (NIV Isa. 52:4). This new revelation—the fact that animals would no longer have to be sacrificed in order to ask for forgiveness—first introduces the idea of people being scapegoats. Ultimately one single person would take on the responsibility of being a living sacrifice for the people of God. Christ ultimately takes all of the sins and infirmities of the world and denies his will in order to pursue his divine calling. This is important and relative to Morrison's text because it is in Geraldine's house (92) when the reader sees a connection between the ultimate scapegoat (Christ) and the scapegoat for that community.

A very blatant example of scapegoating in its most transparent form occurs when Junior invites Pecola into his house to show her Geraldine's cat. After Junior becomes jealous of the affection that his mother's cat is receiving from Pecola (an expression that reminds him of his mother's preference for the cat), he grabs one of the cat's hind legs and he swings the cat around until it is "thrown full force against the window" (91). It is at that moment when Geraldine opens the door and Junior says without hesitation, "She killed our cat" (91). This more litaral example of scapegoating reinforces the tragedy of the character Pecola, as she is deliberately and blatantly blamed for something that she did not do. Even when she is rebuked by Geraldine and told to leave the house, she sees a photograph of Jesus "looking down at her with sad and unsurprised eyes, his long brown hair parted in the middle, the gay paper flowers twisted around his face" (92–93). While the text does not explicitly state why it is that Christ, the ultimate scapegoat, has such an expression on his face, it could mean that Christ understands what it is like to be innocent but to be convicted. There is a parallelism in this section of the text between the two scapegoats, and Morrison establishes a fascinating connection between these two ideas of tragic figures.

Perhaps one of the most important perspectives to take into consideration in the discussion of how Pecola is a scapegoat for others is to consider how she is the scapegoat of Cholly, a man who is not capable of loving but breeding in a dangerous way. Cholly's absent father and his unfortunate first sexual experience results in his inability to connect with his children. "Having no idea of how to raise children, and having never watched any parent raise himself, he could not even comprehend what such a relationship should be" (160). A scapegoat is innocent from the burdens that it carries; similarly, Cholly's "revulsion was a reaction to [Pecola's] young, helpless, hopeless presence" (161). Pecola becomes an emotional dumpster for her father, who is tormented by "hatred mixed with tenderness" (163). She becomes the landfill into which her father pours his previously failed relationships and dumps them literally into her body. This is more than just a metaphorical transference of guilt and shame; this actually becomes a physical penetration, which eventually, she becomes impregnated from. Cholly had been violated psychologically, socially, and personally with the unfortunate hardships that he endured, and he now transfers those same emotions to his daughter when he rapes her.

A scapegoat is someone who bears the blame for the sins, crimes, mistakes, or misfortunes of other people, the individual who suffers in the place of others. The suffering and hopelessness that Pecola endures she cannot control; given her young age, she only internalizes the pain and becomes a product of her destructive environment. Like the scapegoat that she is, Pecola is cast into the wilderness ". . . on the edge of town" (205). Carrying the weight of the burdens for her community, she psychologically loses her sanity because "[a]ll of [their] waste which [the community] dumped on her and which she absorbed . . . all who knew her—felt so wholesome after [they] cleaned [themselves] on her" (205). Pecola is a scapegoat in varying degrees for the people in her community; she is innocent, naive, and unloved. The community "honed [their] egos on her, padded [their] characters with her frailty, and yawned in the fantasy of our strength . . . her guilt sanctified [them]" (205). And though an 11-year-old black girl serves a different function for each individual in the community, she is left to carry the burdens of her society.

WORKS CITED

Holy Bible, The. New International Version. Grand Rapids, MI: Zondervan, 1973.

Morrison, Toni. *The Bluest Eye.* New York City: Plume, 1994.

HOW TO WRITE ABOUT TONI MORRISON

WRITING ABOUT MORRISON: AN OVERVIEW

TONI MORRISON, born Chloe Anthony Wofford in Lorain, Ohio, in 1931, received the Nobel Prize in literature in 1993 for her body of work, at the time making her the eighth woman and the only black woman to receive the prize. The Nobel Committee of the Swedish Academy lauded Morrison as a writer "who in novels characterized by visionary force and poetic import, gives life to an essential aspect of American reality." *Song of Solomon,* her first novel to receive a literary award—the National Book Critics Circle Award in 1977—set a precedent for the acclaim that the rest of her work would receive, and illuminated the two previous works, *The Bluest Eye* and *Sula,* which stand along with *Song of Solomon* and *Beloved* as her greatest works. After the success of *Song of Solomon,* the following year she won the Distinguished Writer Award from the American Academy of Arts and Letters. The acclaimed *Beloved* received the Pulitzer in 1988 and was named the best novel of the past 25 years in 2006 by the *New York Times.* Following the Nobel Prize in literature, in 1994 she received the Pearl Buck Award, and the title of Commander of the Order of Arts and Letters was bestowed on her in Paris. Two years later she received the 1996 National Book Foundation Medal for Distinguished Contribution to American Letters. Reading the works of Toni Morrison and writing about them will take any careful reader and dedicated writer into the vision and poetics of her created worlds that illuminate various American realities with grace and eloquence.

In *The Bluest Eye*, Morrison's first novel and one of her most prominent works, the narrator claims "The pieces of Cholly's life could become coherent only in the head of a musician" (159). This reference to Charles "Cholly" Breedlove provides a wonderful analogy to an interpretation of Morrison's books. Much of her work has a musical quality to it, and many allusions are made to songs and rhythm. As readers, we need to almost suspend belief at times, pay attention to the pieces that are woven together, and read and reread the texts in order to come to a deeper understanding of the work. Morrison's work has been characterized by many literary critics as a challenge for the reader; often the onus is on the reader to interpret events and meanings that can be multiple and layered. There is a lot of work for the reader to do when reading a Morrison text, which makes her work the subject of countless literary theory texts and college and high school papers.

Close reading of the texts gives you an opportunity to investigate the language, ideas, and character development in a piece, and maybe to contrast episodes from text to text, in order to closely study overarching themes in the work. Begin by examining a long passage in a text, identifying metaphors, ideas, and character behavior, and applying the meaning of these to the rest of the novel, if those ideas are repeated throughout the text. Comparing and contrasting passages from different texts make sense if there is a clear reason for the comparison, or maybe if you are setting up an analogy—proving for example that Sethe and Sula appear to be completely different characters, but when analyzed closely, many similarities abound, and it can be seen that they use similar coping methods to deal with their pain of ostracism.

In selecting a section of a novel that you want to examine closely, you may want to consider a subject that is meaningful to you that you can explore further in an essay then find a passage from one of the novels that deals with that subject. In the following passage, Milkman Dead III and Guitar Bains from *Song of Solomon* discuss the plan to steal the gold that they think Pilate Dead is hiding in her house. Guitar feels that Milkman should be assertive and steal the sack without hesitation, instead of thinking of the numerous obstacles that he faces. Guitar admonishes Milkman and encourages him to steal the money by inferring that Milkman is wasting his life:

"Well. If a man don't have a chance, then he has to take a chance!"

"Be reasonable."

"Reasonable? You can't get no pot of gold being reasonable. You have to be unreasonable. How come you don't know that?"

"Listen to me . . ."

"I just quit listening. You listen! You got a life? Live it!" (183)

Guitar's insistence that Milkman take control of his life is an idea that is necessary for the physical and emotional survival of many of Morrison's characters. The ideas in this passage can relate to many characters from Morrison's eight novels. What you would do is find characters who need to live their lives; however, avoid just listing the numerous characters whose lives are stagnant. Rather, relate two or three characters, such as Nel in *Sula,* Denver in *Beloved,* and Christine Cosey in *Love,* and examine their malaise and the ways they are presented in the narrative. The quotation from *Song of Solomon* can be used as a starting point to interpret the three characters' uneasiness with their lives and the actions they make to bring about a change.

A close reading allows us access into the texts to identify ideas for essays. The narrative structure of Morrison's novels can also be analyzed. In a study of Faulkner's and Morrison's fiction, Philip Weinstein concludes that the narrative that is circular in structure—the structure of *Beloved* for example—rather than presented chronologically allows the author to "undo the promise of time by showing effects before causes" (186). The reader often gets a sense of the effect of a particular action, then learns of the root cause later on in the novel. This circularity that many other literary critics have analyzed can be found in many of Morrison's narratives, and could be an interesting way to analyze the novels. The circular narrative allows the reader to experience events multiple times and with varying degrees of intensity, and the narrative often ends where it began, leaving the reader with more insight than at the beginning of the text, although the ending may still be indeterminate. Paying attention to the ways novels begin and end can expose a theme worthy of investigating further.

Song of Solomon begins with Mr. Robert Smith's suicidal flight from a rooftop, and ends with Milkman Dead's literal and figurative flight back to his ancestors, after being violently pursued by his best friend, Guitar Bains. Morrison claims that this circularity and revisiting at the end of the novel allow the reader to become acquainted with the myth of the flying African, one example of the mythology included in her texts. At the beginning of the book, the reader is unaware that Mr. Robert Smith's suicide is because he is a member of the Seven Days—the men who retaliate against white supremacist murders of black people by killing a white person on a given day of the week. When the men can no longer fulfill their mission, they are instructed to kill themselves rather than expose their secret, if the burden of their actions becomes too much and they can no longer continue doing their mission. Therefore the opening suicide, as well as the attempted one by Porter take on new meaning once the secret of the Seven Days is revealed. A writer who looks for important cues at the beginning of the text that the author revisits later on would have a lot of material to work on for an essay.

In her groundbreaking book on Morrison, Trudier Harris identifies a seminal theme in Morrison's work by claiming that "[t]he middle-class status itself becomes a monster for what it represents, not for what it offers, for certainly there is nothing intrinsically negative in a desire for self-improvement. On the path to this kind of self-improvement, however, individuals must give up too much of themselves" (29). This reality of the black middle class is found in characters such as Geraldine in *The Bluest Eye,* Deacon and Steward Morgan in *Paradise,* and Bill Cosey in *Love.* An essay on the black middle class could unearth what these characters sacrifice in order to be successful and if they become alienated from their communities or use their success as a way of negotiating status within the community, as Bill Cosey and the Morgan twins do.

A major theme that can be looked at in every piece of Morrison's fiction is the repercussions of slavery and the internalized racism that often resulted within the African-American community. J. Brooks Bouson states, "*Song of Solomon* is addressed, in part, to middle-class African Americans, especially males, who have a kind of amnesia about their cultural history—about the shame and trauma of family histories rooted in slavery—and who, in donning the mask of bourgeois (white identified) 'pride,' come to see poor blacks as stigmatized objects of contempt" (76). Working around this idea of the shame of a past of enslavement, a writer could explore the way slavery is addressed in other novels, such as *Jazz* and *Beloved.*

In an interview in 2003 on National Public Radio, Morrison said she wants to write from a "strong historical and cultural base in describing what impacts people, especially, maybe exclusively, African Americans." Thus we find another major philosophical idea that is explored in her works: the many African-American experiences in America. This tradition, which could be called revisionist—rewrites the African-American experience in America from the center—from the viewpoint of black people, rather than showing them on the periphery or margins of society. This revision does not mean that black people are described only in positive ways, but rather that their lives and concerns are taken seriously, are multidimensional and complicated the way people's lives are, and are expressed in a way that takes into account the various social and historic forces that have hindered and strengthened the African-American community.

In one of her early interviews in 1983 when Morrison had written four novels, Morrison spoke with the late Nelly Y. McKay, acknowledging, "A writer does not always write in the ways others wish. The writer has to solve certain kinds of problems in writing. The way I handle elements within a story frame is important to me" (142). Here, she is acknowledging the great pressure writers face to satisfy the audience—and the pressure has increased for Morrison since winning the Pulitzer prize and the Nobel Prize in literature. This pressure may have come from the black community to create positive characters who could be interpreted as role models in order to counteract the negative stereotypes of African Americans that were prevalent in the media and fiction. Literary critics apply the pressure also, by fitting her work exclusively into a particular theoretical framework that may not always be applicable, then claiming that she is not successful at mastering that type of writing. A writer could focus on this tension between the author and literary critics. You could also address Morrison's desire to view her writing as a problem to be solved by isolating the elements in her narratives and analyzing the ways the elements deepen our understanding of historical periods or further illuminate character motivation.

In the interview quoted above, Morrison goes on to state, "It's the complexity of how people behave under duress that is of interest to me"

(145). Approaching the novels with that interest in mind would enable you to look at some of her works from that perspective by analyzing the duress that many characters are under. If writing about the obstacles that characters face, you could identify the antagonist, such as the horrors of World War I that Shadrack experiences, or the loss of two sons to the Vietnam War that Deacon and Soane Morgan experience, and then analyze how the character creates a life that helps to assuage the guilt, fear, or pain.

Another way to approach the texts is by looking at the juxtaposition that Morrison states to Nellie McKay: "I want my writing to reflect the imaginative combination of the real world, the very practical, shrewd, day to day functioning that black people must do, while at the same time they encompass some great supernatural element" (153). Novels that do this in particular are *Song of Solomon, Paradise, Tar Baby,* and *Sula.* Take a look at the "supernatural element" in the novel, research the background of the myth—for example the folk tale of the tar baby, or the ghost story as a form in fiction—then relate the element to historical facts if applicable, and the scientific explanations of the element (if any) in contrast to the folktale or mythology.

For most of Morrison's characters, a sense of belonging and fitting into a community is crucial, and is closely linked to racial identity and pride. William "Son" Green asks Jadine Childs in *Tar Baby,* "[Y]ou don't belong to anybody here, do you?" (118). Jadine's search for a sense of belonging as an orphan is a quest that can be found in various configurations throughout Morrison's novels. Milkman's quest for money becomes a quest for wholeness and belonging; Sula's return to the Bottom could be construed as a return to her roots to become part of the community, even though her actions appall and alienate the townspeople.

Morrison's work continues to delight, educate, and challenge those who write about her novels. The many types of characters, narrative structures, and figurative language can be explored in essays. Not all literary critics agree on the various interpretations or assessments of her work. Your job as a writer is not to come up with one infallible approach to the texts but, rather, to see the different ways her work has been interpreted and to perhaps offer one of your own.

TOPICS AND STRATEGIES

Here you will find a variety of topics to consider. The suggestions that follow will give you some ideas about writing about one work as a whole, or on more than one work. The following chapters discuss each individual novel and ways to write about that specific novel; the rest of this chapter takes a broad view of Morrison's work. It is up to you to interpret the events, characters, and ideas in the novels in an original way. Doing your own research can help you to situate some of the occurrences in the novels into historical context and can also help you to identify a unique approach to the novels. Every theme or configuration of ideas is not presented below. What follows are ideas to start your essay-writing process. Many other possibilities exist, since the texts afford you a gamut of ideas to explore further.

Themes

Morrison's novels explore many themes that lead us to contemplate the human condition. Through a close and careful reading of the novels, we can discover the complex nature of parent-child relationships, the significance of physical place to a group of people, the far-reaching effects of a person's dreams, or the role of a specific myth to a cultural group. The previous examples can be delved into when tackling the theme that is inherent in a piece of writing. Memory, friendship, the injustices caused by inequality, the past's influence on the present, and the effects of abuse on both the perpetrator and the victim are integral themes in Morrison's work. Many themes in the books are central to character development, so an exploration of theme in her novels may well be connected to an exploration of a number of characters' lives. Because the themes can be broad topics (violence, love, home, motherhood), try to narrow your focus to a few characters or situations. When writing about Morrison's work in general, make sure your groupings of novels, characters, situations, etc. make sense, and are not simply a random clustering of ideas. You may decide to examine the notion of returning home, and look at the possibility for Jadine Childs in *Tar Baby* and Sula, for example. Ask yourself if the parallel works, what connotations the concept home has for each character, and what are the repercussions or consequences of moving away from one's roots. Analyzing theme should take into account the nuances of each text so that you are not trying to apply one word, like "beauty," to multiple texts in a way that is reductive—reducing the texts to an over-simplified reading.

Sample Topics:

1. **Victims and victimizers:** How does Morrison portray victims and victimizers in her novels? Is either party triumphant in the conflict?

   First you would need to identify the victimizers that are described and the ways they victimize in order to group the characters in some sort of meaningful way. Doing this will help you to avoid simply listing the perpetrators of violence or sexual abuse. Examining the victimizers could lead you to a discussion of the ways that perpetrators of violence are characterized. Often, sexual abusers in Morrison's novels are not one-dimensional monsters. Instead, they are shown suffering greatly (Charles "Cholly" Breedlove), experiencing delusions (Elihue "Soaphead Church" Micah Whitcomb), even being worshipped by others (William "Bill" Cosey). The people on the receiving end of the abuse, in many cases are child victims of sexual abuse: Consolata Sosa, Pecola Breedlove, Seneca, and Heed the Night Cosey. Their powerlessness could be explored, as well as any attempts to retaliate or free themselves from the often life-or-death situation. Because there are so many different forms of abuse, violence, and neglect, like Margaret Street's abuse of her son Michael, Eddie Turtle's action in *Paradise* when he "drove a car over a child and left it there" (133), and Schoolteacher's racially motivated violent acts and beliefs in *Beloved*, you might want to categorize the acts so that your essay is not simply a list of violations.

2. **Friendship:** Examine unlikely friendships and alliances in the novels.

   There are many configurations of friendship in novels such as *Jazz, Love, Song of Solomon, Paradise*, and the short story "Recitatif." An effective way to discuss friendships might be to look at the context that produces the friendship, and if the contexts are similar or noteworthy from novel to novel, then proceed with a discussion of them. You may also consider circumstances that cause the friendship to deteriorate; for example, look at the philosophical differences that cause a rift between Guitar Bains and Milkman Dead. The bonds that transgress lines of race and social class, like the bond shared by Mary "Mother" Magna and Connie, Sethe and Amy Denver, or Twyla and Roberta could be examined by identifying the obstacles the two parties face in their friendship. If the friendship is an example of an unlikely alliance, like that shared between Soane Morgan and Consolata Sosa, or the bond that Alice Manfred and Violet Trace create, ensure that you uncover the meaning of the connection within the context of the novel, and why their relationship is so startling or unique.

3. **History:** In what ways does the past influence the present in the lives of Morrison's characters?

The way Morrison unfolds the past in her fiction could be a starting point in an essay, rather than simply recounting the hidden history. Many characters have deep secrets from the past that imbue them with a sense of shame or keep them from moving forward with their lives. Tied in with the characters' history is their ability or desire to remember the past or the willingness to unearth it. In the Form and Genre section, the characters' quest is explored, and can be connected to their personal history. The past is fundamental to a formation of one's identity: For example, Paul D Garner muses about Beloved, "She reminds me of something. Something, look like, I'm supposed to remember" (234). An essay could argue that many characters are evading a crucial memory, such as Paul D, Sethe, Beloved, Heed the Night Cosey, Christine Cosey, and Deacon Morgan.

4. **Hunting:** Locate the figurative and literal examples of hunting in Morrison's novels, and interpret their significance.

In the broader philosophical context of Morrison's works of fiction, African Americans are fighting to liberate themselves as the quarry of the brutal system of slavery and its far-reaching and equally horrific aftermath. An essay could look at the various characters that are physically and emotionally tormented by this reality, and could explore their success at escaping the reality of living in a society that negates the worth of people based on their race. Another way to approach the topic would be to look at specific instances of actual hunts. Joe Trace in *Jazz* is literally a hunter as a child, learning to hunt from his surrogate father Henry "Hunter's Hunter" Lestory. An adult who cannot reconcile his love for a teenager, he treats Dorcas Manfred as prey (Dorcas in Greek means "gazelle") and hunts and kills her rather than lose her to another man. Milkman is literally hunted by his closest friend Guitar Bains in *Song of Solomon*, and the men of Haven in *Paradise* hunt the Convent women. Link the examples of hunting, whether figurative or literal, and show what the metaphor suggests about the characters or the historical situation.

Character

Morrison's fiction is rich with multifaceted characters that often defy categorization. In some cases it is beneficial to categorize characters from novel to novel to pick up on patterns of human behavior that Morrison is illuminating. The broad categories below allow you as a reader and writer to investigate general character types and to decide whether her characters fit into these distinctions and the purpose in grouping the characters together. The reader is also responsible for making decisions about characters' behavior and for deciding whether or not a character is morally reprehensible, for example. Usually repulsive characters also have redeeming qualities, illustrating the complicated nature of humans, making judgment of these characters complicated. In the novels, the characters, as Morrison has said, face unthinkable hardship and are challenged to cope with tenuous circumstances that can test their humanity. When writing about a character, you may want to identify the struggle the character faces, put it in the context of the novel and the historical context, and uncover the cause and effect of the dire circumstances. Some characters possess mythical powers—such as Baby Suggs in *Beloved*, Marie-Therese Foucault in *Tar Baby*, Pilate Dead in *Song of Solomon*, and Consolata Sosa in *Paradise*. Ensure that any analysis of such traits does not become simply a list of the supernatural occurrences, but a consideration of what the unusual trait or skill means to the character and the community, for example, or how the character uses the trait to help others.

Sample Topics:

1. **The abuser:** How is the abusive character developed and described in Morrison's work?

Writing about an abusive character type might lead to an analysis of the social, historical, and cultural conditions that create such a person. Racial violence in general, sexism, classism, child abuse, the general lack of respect for others—all of these stem from power differentials and could be talked about in an essay. *Paradise* offers many examples of the abuse African Americans suffered in a race and color-conscious society. In deciding where to set up their new town of Haven, the men "discussed . . . the violence of whites, random and organized, that swirled around them" (108). The responses to that racism are interesting, especially if analyzing the internalized racism that leads to further abuse of others within the black community. Other abusers in novels could be examined, such as Bill Cosey in *Love,* Mavis Albright's partner Frank in *Paradise,* and Mr. Henry in *The Bluest Eye.* Again remember to situate the person's actions in a larger context, for example, historical periods gave rise to certain misogynist views of women as property to be owned.

2. **The community:** Identify the role of the community as a character in various novels.

In *Paradise,* Deacon Steward thinks fondly of the old days and thinks the "lazy young. . . . should be chopping, canning, mending and fetching" in service of the community (111). Later on, the attack on the Convent is carried out so that "nothing inside or out rots the one all-black town worth the pain" (5). The fear of the disintegration of the community is palpable in *Paradise.* This privileging of the community and the belonging that people receive from being accepted members could be examined in an essay. All of the novels illustrate the role of the community in African-American life and ways that membership and belonging are essential to people's emotional development. Many novels point out the tragedy when a person is not fully accepted by the larger community. *Sula, Paradise,* and *Love* have interesting examples of this—someone being "put out*doors*" as is stated in *The Bluest Eye,* which connotes being disowned by the group: "if you are outdoors, there is no place to go" (17). The community also functions as a character that coerces others and regulates their behavior, like with the community's rejection of Sethe in *Beloved* and her hurtful withdrawal into isolation, and the community's denunciation of Violet's behavior in *Jazz*.

3. **The renegade:** Many of the novels examine renegade personalities. What role do these people have in the community, and what response do they garner from others?

A writer might discuss the people on the outskirts of society in the terms that Morrison uses in *Paradise.* The men who attack the Convent think of the "detritus: throwaway people that sometimes blow back into the room after being swept out the door" (4). Renegades are often distanced from their families and often desire reconciliation, although Morrison does not use the renegades to glorify families; as L tells us in *Love,* "*Families make the best enemies*" (139). In looking at these people who are on the periphery of society, you might ask what they are escaping from, how the community outcast or rejected them, and if there are any possibilities for reintegration into society. Characters like Circe in *Song of Solomon,* Wild in *Jazz,* and Shadrack in *Sula* seem to be destined to not be a part of "normal" life. Other characters who are not so rejected or isolated, such as May Cosey in *Love* and Violet in *Jazz,* in addition seem to be grappling with psychological troubles that keep them apart from society. Others such as Pilate Dead in *Song of Solomon* and Marie-Therese Foucault in *Tar Baby* deliberately shun the expected ways of existing in the world and have a lot to teach other characters.

4. **The innocent:** Examine the role of the innocent character in Morrison's work.

Because of the subject matter in a lot of Morrison's books, it can be argued that none of her characters is truly innocent when born into the complicated world that humans have created. Starting with defining what it means to be innocent and if people can still maintain their innocence might help to clarify your argument. It remains ambiguous whether or not Shadrack sees Sula and Nel on the afternoon that Chicken Little slips into the river after being spun around by Sula. There are all sorts of implications when exploring who is innocent in that situation. Romen Gibbons saves Pretty-Faye, the girl who is being gang-raped in *Love,* and she seems like the typically innocent character. His actions are admirable, but could he have intervened earlier to save her from so much pain? The writer can also address situations in which people lose their innocence.

History and Context

Since a lot of the events and characters of Morrison's novels are grounded in the historical context of slavery, Reconstruction, and the civil rights struggle, someone who is writing about Morrison's work needs to take into account the historical moment in which she was writing the piece, the historical events mentioned within the text, and the context of the piece of work as it relates to her other works. Some critics claim that Morrison wrote two trilogies, the first includes *The Bluest Eye, Sula,* and *Song of Solomon,* the second consists of *Beloved, Jazz,* and *Paradise.* Forging connections between the texts in each trilogy could produce interesting essays that explore, for example, the different time periods covered and the ways race is dealt with in society in each time period. Interpretations and misinterpretations of history, the diverging ways people remember the same events, and deliberate skewing of history are important philosophical ideas in her work. Writers may additionally situate Morrison's work within the literary tradition of authors such as Virginia Woolf and William Faulkner. Many literary critics see these two authors as the precursors to Morrison's fiction (although Morrison may not agree), and this connection could be explored in an essay.

Sample Topics:

1. **African mythology, Greek mythology, and African-American folklore:** How do African mythology, Greek mythology, and African-American folklore enrich Morrison's narratives?

To write on this broad topic, you might want to narrow the focus to a single mythological framework that Morrison seems to be alluding to or drawing upon to enrich her story. African-American folktales are often referenced, such as the tar baby folktale in Morrison's fourth novel. Rather than noting specific individual instances that seem to be a reference to mythology, try to forge connections between examples so that the references are put into a social or historical context. Rather than simply saying that *Song of Solomon* alludes to Greek and African mythology, you might explore the myths, connect the two (since Morrison could be using a combination of both), and show how the myth illuminates character behavior or motivation. For example, the Greek myth of Icarus, whose overconfidence causes his wings to melt when he flies too close to the Sun, could be the allusion Morrison is referencing in *Song of Solomon*. The main allusion is commonly viewed as the myth of the flying Africans who liberate themselves from a state of servitude. Showing the complexities of the myths and their interpretations and applying them to Milkman's life would deepen the analysis in your essay.

2. **Spirituality:** References to the Bible and other forms of spirituality abound. How are characters' lives influenced or improved by their spiritual beliefs?

A study on spirituality in Morrison's work is so broad that you could find references to talk about in any novel. You could set up contrasting notions of Christianity versus other types of spiritual expression, defining both first. You might also consider approaching the ways Christianity often blends with other forms of religious practices, which was often the case during slavery, when slaves practiced religious syncretism—

praying to traditional African gods while worshipping the Christian trinity and Catholic saints. Many characters have Biblical names—for example characters in *Paradise* and *Song of Solomon*. Try to formulate an argument about the biblical or spiritual reference or practice, for example, the ironies that are apparent within First Corinthians Dead's name and how her personality mirrors the biblical verse.

3. **The legacy of slavery in America:** In what ways does the enslavement of Africans in America affect characters' lives?

When discussing the aftermath of the brutal period of enslavement and its effects on the human psyche, Paul D asks Stamp Paid, "How much is a nigger supposed to take?" (235). These words are jarring for the reader and could elicit a paper about the events that Morrison illustrates that were almost impossible for humans to cope with. Taking history one step further, writers could research life after slavery—during Reconstruction, the two World Wars and the civil rights struggle of the 1960s—to put the events of her novels into historical context. One of the results of institutionalized racism is the occurrence of internalized racism and color consciousness within the black community. What do Morrison's novels such as *Paradise* and *The Bluest Eye* say about the role of internalized racism?

4. **Morrison in the context of other writers and the literary canon:** How do Morrison's novels engage in a conversation with the works of authors whom she is often connected to who may or may not be in the literary canon?

Reading authors such as Alice Walker, Nathaniel Hawthorne, Virginia Woolf, Gloria Naylor, William Faulkner, Ernest Hemingway, James Joyce, Toni Cade Bambara and Gabriel Garcia Marquez can help you to situate Morrison's work within the literary canon. You might also engage in a discussion of the literary canon, and who is traditionally included within it and lauded as a "great author." The resistance that some authors had to the creation and tradition of the canon was that it in some ways excluded authors of color and women writers. Many African-American authors took issue with the selection of literary figures in the canon but decided to continue writing about the issues that they found important to African-American culture, even though that often meant exclusion from the canon. The authors listed above are often referred to as Morrison's contemporaries and/or influences. Identifying specific texts that can be paralleled with Morrison's, for example Alice Walker's *Meridian,* or exploring paralleling narrative forms, such as Garcia's use of magic realism in *One Hundred Years of Solitude* in comparison to Morrison's in *Song of Solomon* could lead to interesting essays.

Philosophy and Ideas

A careful consideration of the social ideas and philosophies that the novels comment on or explore can be an interesting way to approach the texts. Many of Morrison's novels approach problems within American society by examining philosophical beliefs within a society that condoned the system of enslavement of human beings. Another way to look at the ideas in the novels is to analyze characters who seem to be philosophers or thinkers in their own right. Identify those who comment on the fabric of American society and the human condition, for example, then show their impact on other characters or the ways they change their own lives. The character Paul D Garner in *Beloved,* who claims that a rooster named Mister has a better life than he has because the rooster is free, makes a powerful social statement. He realizes the dehumanizing aspects of the system of slavery and takes the enormous risk to escape from Sweet Home after witnessing terrible events. You could also analyze characters who are unlikely philosophers—those on the outskirts of society who exist in the periphery of people's lives, but who nonetheless have significant comments to make about life. Pilate Dead recognizes the importance of human life over the allure of money, and rejects modern society's accepted way of living. Instead, she makes her philosophical choice to privilege family connections over the accumulation of wealth.

Sample Topics:

1. **Resistance to oppression:** How do certain characters resist different forms of oppression?

One way that Morrison revises history is by creating oppressive circumstances for her characters and then having them transcend the subjugation and misery. Examining the resistance to oppression could lead you to uncover the significance of this resistance and under what circumstances the oppression was created. Why is it even important, in that particular context, that the person resisted oppression? In *Paradise*, the oppression characters face comes from many sources—the racist society created by slavery and reconstruction, light-skinned black people in Fairly, Oklahoma, who internalized their oppression, older people in the community who do not want their way of life disrupted, an abusive partner who wants control. Similar examples could be identified in another novel, and the ensuing forms of resistance could be isolated for discussion. In *Paradise*, Mavis Albright resists her violent partner Frank by escaping to the Convent and eventually finding emotional freedom from her abusive past. Unfortunately, before her escape, she leaves her twins, Merle and Pearl, in the car where they suffocate, so that she can attend to Frank's needs. The resistance to oppression, as in this case, may not come early enough to avert tragedy.

2. **Social stratification:** How do characters experience social stratification, and what are the consequences?

You might approach this broad topic by identifying social class differences in a few characters who seem to relate to each other in some way. For example, in *Song of Solomon*, First Corinthians Dead thinks that the women on the bus with her "wouldn't know mediocrity if it punched them right in their fat faces" (196). Her education, which she cannot utilize because of her race, could be explored in comparison to Helene Wright's stultified life in Medallion in *Sula*. You could also examine what Morrison might be saying when she creates characters whose lives are on hold, or who are ridiculed because of their low status. Poverty leads characters to act in desperate ways, as illustrated in *Sula* by Eva Peace's struggle with being a destitute mother and the residents of the Bottom who plunge to their deaths in a sort of protest against the construction company that will not hire them because they are black.

3. **Self-actualization:** Why is self-actualizing important to Morrison's characters?

Major contrasts can be seen in characters who experience a sense of futility in their lives, versus those who have a sense of purpose. First Corinthians's malaise is partly because of a racist society that will not offer her the chance to utilize her education and skills. People often settle into lives that have been hindered by societal roles, and others become angry and make a change in their lives. In *Love,* Christine Cosey tells Heed the Night Cosey about the ways they lacked determination in their lives, "It's like we started out being sold, got free of it, then sold ourselves to the highest bidder" (185). People who do self-actualize, or begin to create an identity and begin to value themselves, often have to do so in the face of overwhelming obstacles. In *Beloved,* Denver starts to think about herself in a new way and muses, "It was a new thought, having a self to look out for and preserve" (252).

Form and Genre

An analysis of the genre or the type of work, in this case fiction, and form, in most cases the novel, can lead to interesting explorations of Morrison's work. Although primarily viewed as a writer of fiction, there are other works that you can access and use in your papers about her writing. Such writings that have garnered critical acclaim are her play *Dreaming Emmett,* appearing on stage in 1986, her book *Playing in the Dark: Whiteness and the Literary Imagination* on literary criticism, and the anthology *Race-ing Justice, En-Gendering Power: Essays on Anita Hill, Clarence Thomas, and the Construction of Social Reality;* the last two books were both published in 1992, the same year as *Jazz.* Morrison herself has resisted her work being put into broad categories, for example, labeling *Beloved* as magical realism because of its supernatural elements. certain elements of that literary form may fit. When looking at the form of the text, try not to immediately categorize it as a modernist text, or a womanist text, for example. Try instead to do what Morrison urges her readers to do—to engage with the text and imagine the multiple possibilities for it, rather than safely securing the work in one literary theoretical framework. As you look from text to text, imagine what the form tells us about the texts and their major themes. In an essay you should look for the many literary devices that the author uses to create and inform the narrative (such as symbols, repetition of words and phrases). Ask yourself questions about the way the narrative is presented to the reader and to characters (in the case of naive characters or narrators, for example). How do we get to see into the characters' minds, and what effect does this have on the reader? What else shapes the story?

Sample Topics:

1. **The quest:** What are many of Morrison's characters on a quest for? Are they successful in their attempts?

   Writing about the quest leaves you with many possibilities, since characters embark on literal and figurative journeys in all of Morrison's novels. You should start with identifying which characters you would like to explore further and your reason for grouping them together across novels. The next step is to discover what the quest says about the character, the situation, society, or the novel as a whole. What is the character escaping from or to? Does the person set off on the journey fully cognizant of his or her actions or what may follow? How is the searcher surprised or transformed by the action? Milkman, for example, leaves town in the quest for gold and ends up recovering a sense of self. When Paul D talks to Sethe about love, the elusive emotion that so many characters are searching for, "[h]e knew exactly what she meant: to get to a place where you could love anything you chose—not to need permission for desire—well now, *that* was freedom" (162). The search for freedom and self-articulation can be related to people's aspiration for self-actualization discussed above.

2. **Point of view:** How does point of view play a role in the unfolding of events?

Writing about point of view in the novels may seem like an overwhelming task, given the various points of view found in just one novel. You could begin with talking about the effect of point of view in general, then move to more specific instances, so that you do not feel obliged to discuss every shift in point of view. Examine the way that the shift exposes different aspects of a person's characteristics or their motivation—the character may withhold information from one person, but divulge all to another character with a shift in point of view, like when Milkman withholds information from Hagar, but the reader is privy to his true feelings about her when he talks to Guitar. Point of view and the ways events unfold can be related to the circular imagery that dominates the narratives in *Paradise* and can be found in *Beloved* and other novels, with more and more information being revealed to the reader and to characters, as if in circles.

3. **Modernism/postmodernism:** How do the literary styles of modernism and postmodernism influence Morrison's work?

You might want to start with a definition of modernism from *The Concise Oxford Dictionary of Literary Terms*, then examine the facets of Morrison's work that could be construed as modernist:

> In fiction, the accepted continuity of chronological development was upset by Joseph Conrad, Marcel Proust, and William Faulkner, while James Joyce and Virginia Woolf attempted new ways of tracing the flow of characters' thoughts in their stream-of-consciousness styles. . . . Modernist writing is predominantly cosmopolitan, and often expresses a sense of urban cultural dislocation. . . . Its favoured techniques of juxtaposition and multiple point of view challenge the reader to reestablish a coherence of meaning from fragmentary forms.

Rather than simply attaching a specific theoretical label to the novels, you might explore aspects of the writing that fit into these categories, then show the effect on the reader or what the technique is illustrating about a character or situation. One way that modernism challenges readers is with a technique that Morrison employs a lot, writing the events of the text out of chronological order, and even leaving out crucial parts of the event until the end of the text when the reader can put it all together.

Postmodernism employs many of the techniques of modernism, but lauds the fragmentary forms in literature. Find novels and narrative patterns that seem to fit the definition (like *Jazz* and *Beloved*); then you could show how the fragmentary memory of Beloved and Sethe illustrates the way lives were fragmented during slavery, for example. In *Jazz*, the dislocation that people experience when migrating to the north, and particularly to Harlem in New York City, seems to be echoed in the fragmentary nature of the text.

4. **Challenging texts:** How do Morrison's texts keep the reader engaged and challenged?

It is almost impossible to read Morrison and understand the text if you are not an active reader. Like in many works of fiction, there are instances in Morrison's work when the characters or the narrator is unreliable, meaning that the reader cannot trust the narrator's interpretation of events. What purpose does this serve? How does Morrison make the reader responsible for the interpretation of many events in the texts? *Paradise*, "Recitatif," and *Love* offer the reader many opportunities to unravel mysteries and layers of meaning in the texts. At the end of *Jazz*, the reader is talked to directly to draw attention to the fact that the reader helps create the reality of the events of a novel. In an essay, you may want to explore the difficulty of two texts, as long as you can connect the challenge in some way, through the themes and the effect on the reader, for example.

Language, Symbols, and Imagery

An author's language choices for particular characters in the story can shed a lot of light on their actions. Look at the way figurative language is used to say something about a situation. Because Morrison's work is full of figurative language, it is easy to point out many examples. Rather than just listing the numerous symbols in stories, try to imagine what the symbols say about certain situations or people, the novels themselves, or the comments Morrison is making about a specific topic or idea. Because of the complex language and symbolic references in the texts, the only way to fully comprehend Morrison novels is to be an active reader—one who fully engages in the language of the text, asking questions, jotting down notes, paying attention to foreshadowing and various other clues of future occurrences in the text and between texts.

Sample Topics:

1. **Pathos: the use of language to elicit an emotional response in the reader:** How does Morrison's language appeal to reader's emotions? What role do emotions play in the lives of characters?

   Some of the events in the novels can take the reader into a painful world of degradation and misery. The texts are replete with emotions that shock or astound and that readers can identify with. Some of the texts also comment on the extent of people's hatred. In *Love*, L asks, "*What good does it do to keep a favorite hate going when the very person you've poisoned your life with is the one (maybe the only one) able or willing to carry you to the bathroom when you can't get there on your own?*" (139). This example illustrates the futility of holding a grudge against someone and insightfully sees people ultimately as connected—even to those they loathe. What a writer should do in writing about pathos is to identify shocking events from novels that are somehow linked and also find examples of extremely powerful language that is utilized in the telling of the event.

2. **Imagery:** Discuss the use of color imagery in the texts.

   Make sure that you have a purpose for unearthing various examples of color imagery. You want to avoid listing images that relate to color in many books without connecting them or revealing their purpose in the context of the novel or the context of the works as a whole. You may discuss imagery in relation to someone's name, for example Golden Gray in *Jazz,* and all the connotations of the name in this historic context. Always contextualize the imagery. In *Beloved,* for example, there is much imagery that refers to the color red, and the various connotations of the color could be explored in the context of the situation in which Sethe, Beloved, and Denver find themselves in. Skin color is an obvious point for discussion, and the ways the character views him- or herself or how others perceive that person.

3. **African-American vernacular and conversation:** How does Morrison create a sense of the complexity of African-American culture through the vernacular and conversation that characters engage in?

Writing about language allows you to study the richness of the words in the novels. One of the foremost ways that people express their identity and sense of belonging to a particular ethnic or social group is through language. You might want to isolate particularly evocative examples that express the character's personality or the interaction that the language fosters. Silence is at the opposite end of this spectrum, and often a character's silence can resound with meaning. Often disenfranchised people are at a loss for words, like when Cholly meets his father and cannot remember his name or when Denver goes to seek help from Lady Jones in the community and can barely articulate her need. Repeated silences are also used as part of the narrative structure—for example the many silences in *Love* and the juxtaposition of sound and silence in *Jazz* add to the form of the novel.

4. **Naming:** In *The Bluest Eye,* Elihue "Soaphead Church" Micah Whitcomb says, "What makes one name more a person than another? Is the name the real thing then? And the person only what his name says?" (180). Discuss these ideas in the context of Morrison's work.

A writer has a lot of material to work with if considering a discussion of naming in the novels of Toni Morrison. Rather than supply a list of interesting names, link the behavior to the name—for example, Deacon and Steward Morgan in *Paradise* are natural leaders, or maybe show the contrast between the name and the behavior of the character—for example, the irony of the Breedloves' name in *The Bluest Eye* and the irony of the place Sweet Home in *Beloved.* Giving people nicknames in an affectionate or critical way is an integral aspect of African-American culture, so the names can be discussed in that context also. In order for your paper to have cohesion, you may want to explore characters whose names can be related in some way or whose names are used by the community in similar ways; for example, in *Jazz,* Violet is condescendingly renamed Violent by the community, and Sydney and Jadine Childs call William "Son" Green "Nigger" in *Tar Baby.*

Compare and Contrast Essays

The books present us with stark contrasts—contrasts that would make for a fascinating essay if explored in earnest. The pitfall to avoid is reducing your essay into a simplistic list of similarities and differences. You can avoid this mistake if you keep your focus on the complexities of certain relationships between opposite individuals or opposing forces. Try to find subtle pairs to compare and contrast from novel to novel, like Pilate in *Song of Solomon* and Therese in *Tar Baby,* or May Cosey in *Love* and Shadrack in *Sula.* First identify what they could possibly have as a basis of comparison. After identifying similarities or differences, examine the characters' roles in the novel and what they represent to members of their communities—ways they are outcast or ways they shun society's rigid restraints, for example.

Sample Topics:

1. *Sula* **versus** *Paradise*: Examine the calm or tranquility that characters experience in contrast to unrest or social upheaval in *Sula* and *Paradise.*

   There are stark contrasts in *Paradise* between the tranquility at the Convent, for example, versus the upheaval brought by the men of Ruby's community who hunt the women and murder them. This reality could be compared to the tranquility the residents of the Bottom feel until Sula appears and disrupts all notions of normality. Of course you would point out any differences between the two cases, and illustrate the ways the unrest informs the reader about the community.

2. **Compare the roles of minor characters:** How do minor characters add complexity to two or more novels?

This broad topic can lead you in many directions. First you would have to isolate a reason why you are discussing these particular minor characters. Maybe they have a lot in common, their characters function in the same way in the text, or maybe you are drawing an analogy—showing how these two characters who appear to be so different are actually quite similar. Minor characters like Tar Baby in *Sula*, Soaphead Church in *The Bluest Eye*, and Lone DuPres in *Paradise* could be examined by contextualizing their behavior, their role in the community and their sense of self.

3. *Jazz* **and** *Love*: Contrast the treatment of different expressions of love in the novels *Jazz* and *Love*.

Writing about these two novels can produce interesting explorations of the way love manifests in characters' lives. The ironic title of the novel *Love* could be explored first and foremost, with the different expressions of love that the women have for Bill Cosey and the underlying hatred for him that is soon apparent. In *Jazz*, people's love for one another also presents itself through contempt or violent acts, as in the case of Joe Trace's feelings for Dorcas Manfred.

4. *Love* **and** *Paradise*: Compare or contrast the role of work in *Love* and *Paradise*.

Work is integral to many characters' lives in the novels. You could begin an essay by identifying the kind of work that the character does or desires to do or is forced to do, and then look at the ways the work or lack thereof illuminates some aspect of the character's life or personality. In *Love,* Bill Cosey is defined by the work he does and the role he takes on in the community—one who provides employment and helps people to remain gainfully employed. Only later do we discover his manipulativeness. In *Paradise,* work defines a generation of individuals and gives them a sense of purpose in life. The women at the Convent shun conventional work and grow vegetables in the garden, which the community folk enjoy, but the women are still ostracized by the community, partly because of the unconventional lives they are leading.

Bibliography and Online Resources

Baldick, Chris. *The Concise Oxford Dictionary of Literary Terms.* New York: Oxford UP, 1991.

Bouson, J. Brooks. *Quiet as It's Kept: Shame, Trauma, and Race in the Novels of Toni Morrison.* Albany: State U of New York P, 2000.

Duvall, John N. *The Identifying Fictions of Toni Morrison: Modernist Authenticity and Postmodern Blackness.* New York: Palgrave, 2000.

Harding, Wendy, and Jacky Martin. *A World of Difference: An-Intercultural Study of Toni Morrison's Novels.* Westport, CT: Greenwood P, 1994.

Harris, Trudier. *Fiction and Folklore: The Novels of Toni Morrison.* Knoxville: U Tennessee P, 1991.

McKay, Nellie Y. "An Interview with Toni Morrison." In *Conversations with Toni Morrison.* Ed. Danille Taylor-Guthrie. Jackson: UP of Mississippi, 1994.

Morrison, Toni. Radio interview with Tavis Smiley Oct. 2003. *Tavis Smiley Show.* Natl. Public Radio. Retrieved 20 Jan. 2007 <http://www.npr.org/templates/story/story.php?storyId=1484643>.

———. *Playing in the Dark: Whiteness and the Literary Imagination.* 1992. Reprint, New York: Vintage, 1993.

———. *Race-ing, Justice, En-gendering Power. Essays on Anita Hill, Clarence Thomas, and the Construction of Social Reality.* New York: Pantheon, 1992.

Taylor-Guthrie, Danille, ed. *Conversations with Toni Morrison.* Jackson: UP of Mississippi, 1994.

Weinstein, Philip M. *What Else but Love? The Ordeal of Race in Faulkner and Morrison.* New York: Columbia UP, 1996.

THE BLUEST EYE

READING TO WRITE

TONI MORRISON's first novel continues to fascinate its readers. It appears on many college syllabi, and remains a staple for discussion and essay topics at the high school and college level. Interest in *The Bluest Eye* (1970) persists because of the timelessness of the multiple plots and characters, the spectacular language and imagery, and the sophisticated narrative that showcases various shifts in point of view. Thematic issues that Morrison's characters face such as domestic violence and self-hatred are found in any racial group or time period; however, these perennial conflicts are mostly generated by the pervasive racism of that specific historical time. The multiple characters whose voices we hear engage us and provide us with a rich, multi-layered narrative to interpret in essays.

In her afterword in 1993, Morrison claims that *The Bluest Eye* is "the public exposure of a private confidence" (214). A writer could utilize Morrison's statement as an entry point into the text by exploring the many instances of personal events that characters experience and/or divulge to the reader. One example of a shameful event is Samson Fuller's stunning rejection of his son, Charles "Cholly" Breedlove. Cholly runs away from home after the death of his Aunt Jimmy, in search of his father who left before he was born; he finds him gambling in Macon and is destroyed by his father's ruthless hostility.

> The man was impatient. "Something wrong with your head? Who told you to come after me?"
>
> . . . he stood up and in a vexed and whiny voice shouted at Cholly, "Tell that bitch she get her money. Now get the fuck outta my face!"

... Cholly sat down on [the sidewalk]. The sunshine dropped like honey on his head.... If he sat very still, he thought, and kept his eyes on one thing, the tears would not come.... While straining in this way ... his bowels suddenly opened up, and before he could realize what he knew, liquid stools were running down his legs. At the mouth of the alley where his father was, on an orange crate in the sun, on a street full of grown men and women, he had soiled himself like a baby (157).

A close reading of a substantial passage such as this one can uncover various topics to consider examining further in an essay. Starting with the betrayal itself, one can begin to piece together Cholly's unfortunate childhood and maybe start to understand his terrible treatment of his own family. He is, of course, responsible for his dire actions later on in life, but the reader can get a sense of the way Cholly's spirit is broken as a child. At a time when Cholly is highly vulnerable (the sole parental figure in his life, Aunt Jimmy, has recently died, and Cholly is left all alone) he sets out to avert his impending fate, believing Darlene may be pregnant, and ends up psychically bruised by his father. He believes his father may have some answers for him, since—years before—his father abandoned his mother while she was pregnant. His childlike belief that finding his father is the answer to his predicament is even more pathetic because Cholly really is all alone in the world with no concrete details about his father, except that he is in Macon. The reader may suspect that Cholly cannot possibly find his father, but incredibly, he finds him quite swiftly. Sadly, Cholly's father is more concerned about his gambling than his own son which illustrates one of the many themes found in the novel— people's desire to avoid poverty. Samson Fuller's one reference to Cholly's beloved Aunt Jimmy is to call her a bitch, and he removes himself from any parenting responsibility because he claims that he has already sent her some money.

This passage also raises central themes that you may want to write about—belonging and abandonment. Cholly, for example, is left with no one who wants to claim him as his or her own. He is now "[d]angerously free.... free to drink himself into a silly helplessness" (159), which he does as an adult, maybe to escape the painful memories of being discarded by his father. Central to his being abandoned is the physical state he finds himself in. He defecates on himself, and sits in his own stench for hours; no one comes to help, and he would probably repel people, as they may mistake him for an alcoholic, which ironically becomes his fate later on in his life.

Being physically desirable to others is another core issue and related theme that Morrison tackles in the book, and is central to this passage. Cholly is unwanted and physically repulsive to the outside world. This theme of perceived ugliness can be applied to almost every character we meet in the novel. The language used to describe Cholly's predicament is noteworthy. Two similes are used—the sun is like honey, and seems to conjure up a sense of his being soothed and loved by the universe, and he is like a baby who has dirtied his diaper, but without a parent to care for him and caress him, the way the sun does. Morrison divulges to the world the effects of Cholly's painful moment of shame, which reverberates throughout the text and touches other characters' lives.

The Bluest Eye is often noted as the most accessible of Toni Morrison's novels, but a writer still has to take the time to reread the text and to delve deeper into the issues raised by certain character's actions, such as child neglect and abuse. Being an active reader—one who asks questions of the text and engages with the text at all levels—helps when transferring ideas about the novel to the page. There are many approaches to the novel, and the vast amount of scholarship on the book has a lot to offer any writer who wants to carefully consider the ideas in the text.

TOPICS AND STRATEGIES

Here you will find a variety of topics to consider. It is up to you to interpret the events and characters in the novel in an original way. Doing your own research can help you to situate some of the occurrences in the novel into historical context and can also help you to devise a unique approach to the novel.

Themes

Many themes in the book are central to character development, so an exploration of themes in *The Bluest Eye* may well be connected to an exploration of a number of characters' lives. A writer might want to start by locating and identifying an idea in the novel and following that idea throughout the novel, noting its impact on character development. For example, early on in the book, the reader comes to understand that beauty is important to Pecola and other characters. That theme can be followed and connected not only to the character's beliefs about beauty but to the role society plays in personal reflections about beauty and worthiness. Although this book is narrated by a child and focuses in depth on another child's life, it is not a children's book; the themes are mature and complex and worthy of further investigation. Once you have identified a theme, decide what the novel is saying about it. Innocence and the corruption of innocents in the novel is a major theme. Go further than simply identifying the theme by perhaps asking who is responsible for protecting the innocent members of society and if anyone in the novel effectively protects vulnerable characters.

Sample Topics:

1. **Perceptions of ideal beauty and ugliness:** In what way is this novel a commentary on beauty and ugliness and people's commonly warped perceptions of both?

   "Except for the father, Cholly, whose ugliness (the result of despair, dissipation, and violence directed towards petty things and weak people) was behavior, the rest of the family—Mrs. Breedlove, Sammy Breedlove, and Pecola Breedlove—wore their ugliness, put it on, so to speak, although it did not belong to them" (38). An essay on beauty could begin with an analysis of this powerful summation of the self-loathing that Pecola Breedlove is mired in. Characters other than Pecola also struggle with their physical appearance and could be carefully analyzed.

2. **The innocence of childhood and coming of age:** Think about how childhood is represented in the novel. How do the interactions between Claudia MacTeer and her sister Frieda contribute to the themes of the novel and of what it means to be a child?

   Writing about childhood may include how the narrator Claudia and her sister Frieda try to make sense of their world; as they listen to the adults around them, they must "listen for truth in timbre" (11). Their childlike perspective on the world is instantly recognizable, for example, when Claudia "began to concentrate on the white spots on [her] fingernails. The total signified the number of boyfriends [she] would have. Seven" (27). Moments like this one, where the narrator makes sense of her life in childlike ways can be read in contrast to the many cases of child abuse, a theme detailed below.

3. **Child abuse/incest:** What leads to child abuse and/or incest in the book? What motivations does Morrison provide for the characters' despicable actions?

An essay focused on the novel's abuse might allow you to analyze characters who are not as obvious as others. Two secondary characters with whom Pecola comes in contact—Geraldine, "the pretty lady" (94), and Elihue "Soaphead Church" Micah Whitcomb—have lasting effects on her self-esteem, and represent adults with the ability to irrevocably damage children. These and other instances of blatant or subtle exploitation could be systematically examined.

Character

Luckily for the reader, Morrison fully develops many characters in this novel, which means that you are not restricted to examining only one or two "main" characters. A detailed essay could be written about almost every character that appears in the book, including those on the periphery. The book is decidedly character driven, but characters and their actions are closely connected to the themes and comments that Morrison makes about society and human behavior. The novel illuminates the damaging effects of society on the individual and holds many accountable for people's suffering: institutionalized racism, ill-equipped parents, and malevolent personalities.

Sample Topics:

1. **Pecola Breedlove's character:** Why is Pecola Breedlove so consumed by a conscious and unconscious self-hatred?

To begin to consider writing about Pecola, one could turn to the fact that, in the novel, her name references the character Peola Johnson, the light-skinned daughter of housekeeper Delilah Johnson in the 1934 film *Imitation of Life*, who resents her mother's dark skin and eventually passes for white. The tragedy in Pecola Breedlove's mind would be that she cannot possibly pass for white or for someone who is, she believes, truly beautiful.

2. **Minor characters:** Examine the role of three minor characters in the novel.

Minor characters such as Geraldine, Elihue "Soaphead Church" Micah Whitcomb, Mr. Yacabowski, and the prostitutes (China, Poland, and Miss Marie) all play substantial roles in Pecola's life. Morrison also uses these characters to extend the scope of the novel. Soaphead Church's part in the novel includes a letter that he writes to God, which adds another dimension to the narrative. The letter provides insight into the mind of a child molester whose horrific acts leave us dumbfounded. What does Morrison's inclusion of this character add to the themes of the novel?

3. **Charles "Cholly" Breedlove's character:** Cholly Breedlove's character is multifaceted and his actions are chilling and disturbing. How does Morrison create a character who is simultaneously fascinating and repelling?

As you write, keep in mind Morrison's words from the afterword that refer to her reluctance to "dehumanize the characters who trashed Pecola and contributed to her collapse" (211). As a 14-year-old boy, Cholly "cultivated his hatred of Darlene. . . . The one whom he had not been able to protect" (150), which could be interpreted as perhaps the beginning of his misogyny, violence, and self-contempt. Cholly's painful existence as a child could be explored in an essay and linked to his failure to value others around him, even his relatives.

History and Context

This book was published in 1970, at a time when African Americans were still not being viewed seriously in America as artists and when they were often expected to write solely about the African-American experience (which was defined quite narrowly). The events in the novel are astonishing in their repugnance, and later authors such as Alice Walker experienced the backlash aimed at authors who wrote about the underbelly of African-American culture, exposing realities such as incest and domestic abuse. Morrison truly was taking a brave step forward by publishing a book examining such topics as incest and child abuse; many people were not ready for African Americans to be written about in a negative way, as it could reinforce negative views of African Americans. All of these issues can be explored further in an essay that deals with the novel's history and context.

Sample Topics:

1. **The impact of media figures such as Shirley Temple on a race-conscious society:** How does Shirley Temple's brief mention at the beginning of the novel frame the novel's social critique about white supremacy and how it creates conceptions of ideal beauty?

   "Adults, older girls, shops, magazines, newspapers, window signs—all the world had agreed that a blue-eyed, yellow-haired, pink-skinned doll was what every girl child treasured" (20). Claudia's outlook on the racially biased ideal of beauty is a fascinating one that could lead to an in-depth discussion in an essay. Despite her youth, she tries to resist the pressure to be drawn into worship of such ideals, although she does concede, "I learned much later to worship [Shirley Temple] . . . even as I learned, that the change was adjustment without improvement" (23).

2. **The effects of racism and internalized racism in America:** Although the novel is timeless, Morrison is writing about a specific historical period in which there was legally sanctioned segregation in America and legally sanctioned discrimination

based on race. How does this background play a role in an understanding of the characters' struggles?

Morrison clearly identifies the effects of racism in the character of Geraldine, who in turn teaches her son the intricacies of race and by doing so reinforces racist traditions: "She had explained to him the difference between colored people and niggers. . . . Colored people were neat and quiet; niggers were dirty and loud" (87). When Cholly experiences the callous side of the racist society he is a part of, he takes the harsh treatment from the ticket man at the bus station "at the colored side of the counter" (152) with ease, since "[t]he insults were part of the nuisances of life, like lice" (153). How do situations like these have a compounding negative effect on the characters?

3. **African-American women's historical domestic role:** How does Morrison portray African-American women's roles in the 1930s and 1940s?

To answer this broad question, you could do further research on the topic and incorporate it into your essay by turning, for example, to Paula Giddings's *When and Where I Enter: The Impact of Black Women on Race and Sex in America,* which puts into historical context the work of African-American women. In *The Bluest Eye,* we see the domestic employment these women engaged in and the impact, for example, that Pauline Breedlove's status as a maid has on her family: "More and more she neglected her house, her children, her man— they were like afterthoughts" (127). Why might her job have led her to such neglect?

Philosophy and Ideas

The book is rich with philosophical ideas and philosophical musings on the nature of human behavior. Morrison's novel presents us with many opportunities to gaze inside the lives of those whom society would deem a menace to its very fabric. For example, *The Bluest Eye* allows us into the minds of child molesters, maybe so that we can condemn their actions further, or so that we can consider what creates such abhorrent behavior. It is up to you as a reader of Morrison's work to form your own opinion and create your interpretation in your essays of the treacherous actions of such individuals.

Sample Topics:

1. **Adult treatment of children:** How do adults regard or disregard children in the novel?

   To explore this topic, you could turn to Claudia's early descriptions of her daily life and what they tell us about the ways adults regard children. She says, "Adults do not talk to us—they give us directions" (10), and that children are "merely pointed out" to Mr. Henry (15). Later on, when we read of Cholly's upbringing, we read, "Nobody talked to him; that is, they treated him like the child he was" (140). What other instances of adults dismissing children do we encounter in the book, and what impact does this have on those children?

2. **The archetypal "perfect" family:** Why does Morrison juxtapose the Dick and Jane story to the Breedloves' family life?

   The opening Dick and Jane narrative that frames each section on the Breedlove family is hard to miss and appears in ironic contrast to the Breedloves' family life. The Breedloves defy the rules of the community by not quite fitting in, which can be discussed in an essay about belonging (see below). A neighbor remarks on this by saying, "Don't nobody know nothing about them no way. . . . Don't seem to have no people" (189). Instead of being the image of perfection like the family in the Dick and Jane storybooks, the children in families like the Breedloves "were everywhere. They slept six in a bed, all their pee mixing together in the night as they wet their beds each in his own candy-and-potato-chip dream" (92). Poverty, deprivation, literal and figurative hunger—these are all issues you could explore further in an essay on images of family life, not forgetting, of course, their ironic family name.

3. **People's sense of belonging and ownership:** What is the importance of the ways belonging and ownership are described in the novel?

A desire to belong is a central philosophical theme running throughout the novel. People want to belong, and they want to matter to someone other than themselves. There are many factors that can lead to belonging or ostracism. As a child, Pauline Williams's deformed foot causes her to "never feel at home anywhere, or that she belonged anyplace" (111). Integral to belonging is ownership. If characters own a house or property, then they have a reason to exist, and will not face the fearsome fate of being displaced: "If you are outdoors, there is no place to go," (17) explains the narrator, Claudia MacTeer. There is also the fear of belonging to an undesirable group; Pecola Breedlove realizes "[a]s long as she looked the way she did, as long as she was ugly, she would have to stay with these people. Somehow she belonged to them [her family]" (45).

Language, Symbols, and Imagery

Because of the complex language and symbolic references, the only way to fully comprehend this and other Morrison novels is to be an active reader—one who fully engages in the language of the text, asking questions, jotting down notes, and paying attention to foreshadowing and the establishing and extending of themes in the text. Reading *The Bluest Eye* for the language alone is a rewarding experience, and focusing in on the language could produce a remarkable essay. You could examine African-American vernacular, the way people converse with each other, the imagery, symbols, and the ways characters use language to describe themselves, like Pauline Breedlove's first-person recollections of her life, or Soaphead Church's letter to God.

Sample Topics:

1. **Figurative language: metaphors/similes/personification/ symbols:** How does the figurative language help to create a sense of the narrators' lives?

   In your essay you could examine the breathtaking language in Morrison's first novel. Various metaphors, similes, symbols, and personification infuse the novel and continue to delight readers. You may want to consider the way Pauline bears her husband "like a crown of thorns, and her children like a cross" (127) while she continues to lose her teeth and any semblance of beauty that the "painted ladies" (126) possess. The comparisons work so well because Pauline becomes a martyr who almost relishes the battles with her alcoholic husband. Make sure you relate the figure of speech to the character's personality or motivation to behave in a particular way, rather than simply pointing out the language itself.

2. **Allusions:** Explore the opening "Dick and Jane" section and relate it to the lives that the narrators and the community people actually lead.

   This opening is unique, as are the openings of all of Morrison's novels, and has sparked much discussion. Is Morrison's allusion to the Dick and Jane storybook a claim that the characters are unrealistic and that no one can possibly create such a family system, or is she trying to illustrate how racism combined with poverty can destroy families, depriving them of a chance to flourish?

3. **Conversation:** Give examples of how "conversation is like a gently wicked dance" (15) in the novel and how it bonds people or destroys relationships.

   For an essay about conversation, you have many rich examples to choose from. The conversation between the family and friends of Cholly's dead Aunt Jimmy is replete with insights into the corruption present in modern life, such as the fraudulence of some insurance companies. The conversations that the three prostitutes have that Pecola listens to are also telling. In the banter among the women, Pecola finds lessons on how to be a woman, and often hears comments that are inappropriate for a young girl to muse about.

Compare and Contrast Essays

A useful approach to an essay is to identify parts of a story and analyze their similarities or differences. Pecola Breedlove's naïveté and innocence could not be a greater contrast to Soaphead Church's worldliness and malfeasance, this is an example of the sharp contrasts in Morrison's first novel. You might want to consider what Morrison is saying about Pecola Breedlove's world that contains such contrasts in moral and ethical behavior and the impact this world has on the innocent members of this society. In such an essay, it is important that you try not merely to list what two characters or situations have in common or how they differ; instead, relate your discoveries to an aspect of society that may be responsible for their behavior, for example. You can also consider the similarities from novel to novel because many connections have been drawn between *The Bluest Eye* and Morrison's other novels. *The Bluest Eye* can be compared and contrasted to *Sula, Beloved,* and *Love* in their depictions of motherhood, the impact of the narrative voice, the role of the family, the effect of child abuse on its perpetrators, and the way society pressures the individual.

Sample Topics:

1. **Claudia MacTeer versus her sister Frieda MacTeer:** How different are Claudia and her sister?

   Morrison contrasts the narrator and her sister, and presents us with a looking-glass into the nuances and confusions of childhood. At the beginning of the novel, Claudia is "[s]ick and tired of Frieda knowing everything" (28), and at the end, what they have in common is that they are both in the dark about why Pecola became and remained a victim. Why does Morrison allow both the narrator and her sister to remain in ignorance?

2. **Pauline Breedlove versus Charles "Cholly" Breedlove:** Examine the nature of the volatile relationship that the husband and wife share and what creates their distinct personalities.

   Pauline Breedlove is described as "the ideal servant" (128) by her employers, Mr. and Mrs. Fisher, yet she remains thoroughly disappointed by her life, as does Cholly (42). How does Cholly feel about his life? You may also turn to the fact that they seem to save each other from the harsh realities of their lives, but the end result is quite chaotic.

3. **Pecola Breedlove versus Claudia MacTeer:** In what way does Claudia manage to survive the hostile racist world in which she lives, in ways that Pecola is unable to do?

   For an essay on this intriguing topic, you could consider the familial or communal support each girl has, or the lack thereof. You may want to incorporate a discussion of belonging and abandonment, and the impact both have on the characters' ability to self-actualize. It is interesting to note that Claudia's father goes unmentioned, in contrast to Pecola's complicated father whose actions are devastating and far-reaching.

4. **The Individual versus the Community:** What price do characters pay for not fitting into the community?

   You could examine the role of the three prostitutes, the Breedlove family, and others who are on society's margins. Investigate the way Morrison comments on those who conform and those who disregard social rules. What do both the conformists and the nonconformists suffer because of their choices? Does Morrison set up a dichotomy regarding what people should do, or are choices more complicated? Because incest is a part of their family legacy, the Breedlove family, for example, loses the favor of the community. They are pitied and scorned, and the children (who did not choose the behavior, hence the dilemma of either conforming or not) seem to suffer the most from the family being ostracized.

Bibliography for *The Bluest Eye*

Alexander, Allen. "The Fourth Face: The Image of God in Toni Morrison's *The Bluest Eye*." *African American Review* (Summer 1998): 293–303.

Bloom, Harold, ed. *Toni Morrison's* The Bluest Eye. Bloom's Modern Critical Interpretations. Philadelphia: Chelsea House Publications, 1999.

de Weever, Jacqueline. "The Inverted World of Toni Morrison's *The Bluest Eye* and *Sula*." *CLA Journal* 22 (1979): 402–14.

Fick, Thomas H. "Movies, Consumption, and Platonic Realism in *The Bluest Eye*." *MMLA* 22 (Spring 1989): 10–22.

Gates, Henry Louis, Jr., and K. A. Appiah, eds. *Toni Morrison: Critical Perspectives Past and Present*. Amistad Literary Series. New York: Amistad P, 1993.

Giddings, Paula. *When and Where I Enter: The Impact of Black Women on Race and Sex in America*. New York: William Morrow, 1984.

Harris, Trudier. *Fiction and Folklore: The Novels of Toni Morrison*. Knoxville: U of Tennessee P, 1991.

Moses, Cat. "The Blues Aesthetic in Toni Morrison's *The Bluest Eye*." *African American Review* (Winter 1999): 623–37.

Ogunyemi, C. O. "Order and Disorder in Toni Morrison's *The Bluest Eye*," *Critique* 19, no. 1 (1977): 112–20.

SULA

READING TO WRITE

Toni Morrison's novels are well known for being complex and challenging pieces of fiction that can be interpreted in a range of ways. Keep this in mind as you read *Sula* and think about your essay topic. One of the ways *Sula* challenges the reader is by the ambiguous nature of characters' actions and life choices. Why does Morrison seemingly leave the reader with the responsibility for deciding whether certain actions are morally correct? In what ways does she present us with a character's decision without judging the behavior? Examining what motivates characters can lead to many interesting discussions in an essay about the town of Medallion, its inhabitants, and the historical time period.

Close reading of a section of the novel can help you to identify an angle to take in your essay. We will now closely analyze the heated emotional exchange between Eva and her daughter Hannah, to begin to discover a choice of topics to write about. The conversation provides one of the moments in the book when characters are forced to consider their actions and have to provide an explanation for their behavior:

> "Wasn't nobody playin' in 1895. Just 'cause you got it good now you think it was always this good? 1895 was a killer, girl. Things was bad. Niggers was dying like flies. . . . With you all coughin' and me watchin' so TB wouldn't take you off . . . what you talkin' bout did I love you girl I stayed alive for you can't you get that through your thick head or what . . . ?". . .
>
> "But what about Plum? What'd you kill Plum for, Mamma?". . .
>
> "I done everything I could to make him leave me and go on and live and be a man but he wouldn't and I had to keep him out so I just thought

of a way he could die like a man and not all scrunched up inside my womb, but like a man" (72).

The dialogue allows us to uncover the sense of abandonment that Hannah feels; we can also appraise Eva's morally ambiguous justification for killing her own son Ralph, known as Plum. As readers we catch a glimpse of the rationale behind the act of mercy killing that Eva engages in when she sets her son alight. We are left to evaluate her actions for ourselves, which could lead to an interesting exploration in an essay on parental responsibilities and ethical behavior.

The metaphor that Eva uses to describe Plumb's drug-addled state is extremely powerful. She compares him to a baby who wants to return to the womb. His unnatural desire is compounded by her repetition that he is a "big old growed-up man," thus allowing us to internalize the fact that he is a person beyond help, who cannot be roused out of his permanent child-like state which is brought on by his extreme drug addiction. How is the reader affected by Morrison's use of vivid imagery ("scrunched up inside my womb"), figurative language (the personification of Tuberculosis), African-American vernacular ("Wasn't nobody playin'"), and references to social inequalities and poverty ("Niggers was dying like flies")? When writing your papers, including these considerations can greatly enhance your analysis.

In the conversation between Eva and Hannah, Morrison presents us with bizarre events in her characters' lives in a way that is plausible to the audience. This is typical of Morrison's work, and essential in great fiction—the crafting of peculiar events in a way that the audience can relate to and actually believe. These odd events can be explored further as you begin to write, and can provide many ideas for essays. In your essays you may want to ponder the questions: How does Morrison get the reader to suspend disbelief? How are we so effectively drawn into her fictional world? Some other examples of the bizarre in the novel that can be written about are the three boys whom Eva names Dewey who remain 48 inches tall, the mystery of Eva's missing leg, the plague of robins that announce Sula's return to the Bottom after her 10-year absence, the death of Chicken Little, and the ball of fur that accompanies Nel after her husband betrays her. Is the world Morrison creates unbelievable, or do stranger events occur in the real world? An in-depth analysis of *Sula*'s multi-layered narrative can produce thought-provoking essays and discussions; the following section will offer some specific suggestions for essay topics.

TOPICS AND STRATEGIES

Here you will find a variety of topics to consider. It is up to you to interpret the events and characters in the novel in an original way. Doing your own research can help you to put some of the occurrences in the novel into historical context, and can also help you to identify a unique angle to the novel to address in your paper.

Themes

The themes in the novel are numerous and could lead to thought-provoking papers. An obvious choice is friendship, but looking further into the novel may help you to avoid writing on a theme that has been excessively analyzed. Contemplate recurring ideas running through the narrative that strike your curiosity. Beauty, individualism, war, peace, morality—these are some themes that can be fleshed out to generate a remarkable essay. An exploration of peace, for example, could lead you on a literary journey that considers the irony of the family name Peace, characters' futile search for a sense of peace, and the apparent peacefulness (or monotony) of life in Medallion before Sula's return. Find the places in the book that wrestle with the issue, and note characters' reactions to the issue or the way it is manifested in the story. You may ask yourself what Morrison is doing by revisiting this idea throughout the novel—is she commenting on societal norms? Is she using a character to reject these norms or expectations? Themes often overlap with philosophical ideas, so do not limit yourself to writing about one word that you imagine represents the whole book, like beauty. Stretch yourself to consider other possibilities such as the role of racism and internalized racism in people's perceptions of beauty.

Sample Topics:

1. **Individualism:** How do people who are staunchly individualistic (for whatever reason) fare in the novel? Is it possible to break away from the tediousness of the collective and to be one's own person?

There are many characters to write about who live solitary lives, in spite of the collective pressure from the community members of Medallion. Sula is resolutely individualist and claims she does not need the community for her survival. In contrast, her grandmother Eva survives because of gifts of food from community members. Sula abhors the notion of slipping into anonymity, like the rest of the community, whereas Nel cannot imagine not belonging to the collective. Other characters to consider for an essay on individualism: Shadrack, Helene Wright's mother, Tar Baby, Plum.

2. **Violence:** What role does violence play in the lives of the inhabitants of Medallion? Are the violent deaths extreme or realistic?

Almost every character in the novel has some sort of brush with violence, so there is plenty to write about for an essay on this topic. You also need to keep in mind the complexities of the violence to avoid creating a laundry list of violent acts in your paper; simply listing violent occurrences is not analyzing, which is what you want to do when writing. Look at the range of emotions involved in various violent acts or thoughts: Nel remembers that she feels joy at Chicken Little's disappearance in the river, Sula tells her grandmother to be cautious because she may set her on fire when least expected, Shadrack watches as the people on his National Suicide Day parade succumb to the icy depths of the river and drown.

3. **Love:** In what ways is the love in the novel a salve for the many horrific occurrences? How is the love not enough to appease the characters in light of their extreme suffering?

As with writing about violence, do not neglect the range of emotions involved in the different kinds of love present in the book: Eva's endowment to her daughters was the gift of loving men, Jude wants to marry to make him whole, whereas years later Nel's love for Jude had not made her a better person, but "had spun a steady web around her heart" (95). Try not to simplify this topic, since it is one that can initially be appealing to write about because it may seem an easy subject to tackle. You can maintain the complexity if you reflect on the less obvious examples of love, and try to discover people's motivations. Interpreting ironic statements about love might be a place to begin for an essay. What can you say about the way Ajax proclaims "[A]ll [women] want . . . is they own misery. . . . Ax em to die for you and they yours for life" (83)?

Character

At first glance, Shadrack, Sula, and Nel appear to be the main characters of the book. Some critics claim that the people of Medallion are also a main character, and that they make up a collective protagonist. Approaching the novel in this way in an essay might be appealing. How do Medallion's townsfolk collectively become a character? Do they all think alike? Who lies on the outskirts of the unit, and why? Returning to the themes in the novel will help you when drafting your ideas on character. You can ask yourself why certain characters feel the need to distance themselves from the group and how societal norms such as racism, classism, and sexism unite some characters or stifle others.

Sample Topics:

1. **Nel Wright's character:** Discuss the following quotations in an essay: when Nel proclaims, "I'm me. I'm not their daughter. I'm not Nel" (28) and the narrator's observation about Nel that "[h]er parents had succeeded in rubbing down to a dull glow any sparkle or splutter she had" (83). What role do parents have in shaping their children? Is it possible to distance oneself from high parental expectations?

   Analysis of carefully chosen quotations can produce remarkable essays. For this essay you could show that Nel has exhibited some rebellious characteristics, but is still a conformist. Her rebellious nature allows her to understand Sula's shortcomings without going as far as the rest of the community by labeling her as evil. You could research the effects of parental pressure on children and incorporate those facts into your discussion.

2. **Sula Mae Peace's character:** How does Sula conflict with the inhabitants of Medallion while asserting herself as a unique individual?

For your essay, think of the situation when Sula tells her grandmother that she wants to create herself. How does she accomplish this feat of self-creation? What is the effect on Sula when she hears her mother say she loves her, but does not like her? Is it ironic that Sula "helped others define themselves" (95)? Since "[t]hey believed that she was laughing at their God" (115), she certainly helps the town define evil. Why is her "indifference to established habits of behavior" (127) a reason for the town to hold her in such disregard?

3. **Shadrack's character:** What does Shadrack's character teach us about the after effects of war and the ways mentally ill people can be ostracized from a community?

Morrison's portrayal of Shadrack's post-traumatic stress disorder after his experiences in World War I is a most touching account of the struggle to retain equilibrium after the shocking events of war. Your essay could encompass his difficult struggle to maintain a sense of stability and to keep loneliness and dejection at bay; you could also address how successful he is at creating stability and fending off loneliness. How does he regain a sense of normalcy in spite of being viewed as a vagrant in Medallion? Why do people join him finally in his National Suicide Day march in 1942?

History and Context

In the 1970s many African-American authors faced extreme pressure from society to write about the stereotypical African-American experience, which was often interpreted as the effects of racism on the black community. Because the country was reeling from the aftermath of brutal racism which led to the Civil Rights Movement, people expected artists and writers to address these issues in their work. Morrison talks about these demands in the foreword of *Sula*. Never one to conform to external pressure, Morrison addressed the black experience in a unique way, focusing instead on women's relationships and dysfunctional family connections. Writing about the historical context that produced *Sula* can take you in many directions, to the racial injustice that Ajax refers to as "the natural hazards of Negro life" (133), the influence Christianity has on the black community, and the treatment of black women who society claims, "[c]an't have it all" (142).

Sample Topics:

1. **World War I:** War is the backdrop for many works of fiction. How do the events of World War I frame the novel and lead us into the often violent world in Medallion? Is *Sula* an anti-war novel?

   This essay could use Shadrack's experiences to present a clear argument on whether or not you think the novel actually portrays war in such a way as to make a stance against it. In what ways does Shadrack survive the war physically, but not emotionally? How successful is he at making a safe haven for himself? You could look into the treatment that veterans faced after the war and compare Morrison's portrayal of Shadrack to historical accounts.

2. **Racism in America:** How do some of the characters in the novel experience racism?

   There are blatant forms of racism in Sula's world, but Morrison also presents the subtleties and complexities of racism that can be missed with a cursory look at the book. The blatant examples that you could write further on are the Sheriff's shocking comment to the bargeman who finds Chicken Little to throw the body back into the river, the difficulties the Medallion men have in securing work, and the townspeople's rage which leads to several of them drowning in the tunnel on National Suicide Day in 1942. A subtle or complex example might be the way Nel's mother Helene Wright makes her pull her nose so that she can "have a nice nose" (55) and be beautiful. In an essay you could explore the role that societal racism plays in Helene's internalized racism.

3. **The role of Christianity in African-American fiction:** Explore the functional role of Christianity and the spirit world in the novel. Why do Medallion's inhabitants have a "simple determination not to let anything . . . keep them from their God" (150)?

Addressing such a broad topic as Christianity in the novel is quite an undertaking. You could write a lengthy research paper on the topic, or limit yourself to a few examples of the power of Christianity in the lives of Medallion's inhabitants. Exploring the way Christianity placates people from the harsh reality of racism or the brutal events in life, such as Chicken Little's inexplicable death or Hannah's tragic death, might be an interesting focus. What other kinds of spiritual strengths do people draw on? Why are the townsfolk so determined to label Sula as evil?

Philosophy and Ideas

Much of Sula's conversation consists of philosophical musings about human nature, responsibilities to the community, gender expectations, and moral dilemmas. In your essay, an examination of Sula's beliefs and other characters and their philosophies might uncover varied approaches to living (and dying). Why does Morrison use characters such as Ajax, Shadrack, and Helen Wright to represent the world of Medallion? Is there any juxtaposition of philosophies that allow us to examine our own beliefs and worldviews?

Sample Topics:

1. **Alienation caused by abandonment:** In what ways are many characters in the novel alienated from the collective? How do they cope with their loneliness, their preoccupation, and other after effects of feeling abandoned?

Sula's profound loneliness would make for a compelling essay. What is ironic about her loneliness, given that she is bored so easily by others and refuses to conform, even if she will have no friends? How do the people of Medallion manage to maintain a sense of hope in the face of racism and abandonment by society at large? Answering these questions will lead you to a synthesis of the numerous personal struggles that people have in the novel when feeling abandoned.

2. **Ethical behavior:** The townsfolk of Medallion are shocked and disturbed when Sula puts her grandmother, Eva, in a nursing home. Find other examples of dishonorable behavior, include who defines the behavior as unethical, and explore people's responses to it.

   There are many examples of unethical behavior in the novel. What do you make of the fact that Sula watches her mother burn to death with interest? What about the silence that Nel and Sula uphold after Sula drops Chicken Little in the river and he drowns? Are the community members morally responsible for remaining silent about Tar Baby's excessive alcoholism? These and other questions could be argued in a fascinating paper on ethics in *Sula*.

3. **The search for self-knowledge:** How does Shadrack's journey of self-discovery evolve after his tragic experiences in World War I? Discuss the journey of self-discovery for three other characters in the book.

   In an essay about Shadrack, we could view him as a symbol of the struggle that Medallion's community faces. He is the gaping wound that people in the community think they are immune from, but which they also suffer greatly from. What journeys do other characters embark on in their quest for self-knowledge (or their desire to remain in denial)?

Language, Symbols, and Imagery

Morrison's novels are well known for their dazzling images and lyrical qualities. *Sula* is no exception, and an essay built around the well-crafted poetics of people's conversations would make for fascinating reading. It is easy for an essay on figurative language to deteriorate into a list of symbols and metaphors. One way to avoid this pitfall is to ask what the symbols mean in the larger context of the book. You can uncover, for example the meaning of the grey ball of fluff that Nel sees and that eventually dissipates when she realizes it represents her sorrow over losing her soul mate Sula. So rather than simply pointing out a figure of speech or a clever play on words, relate it to a character or to the historical or social context.

Sample Topics:

1. **Figurative language: metaphors/similes/personification/ symbols:** The figurative language prevalent in *Sula* adds a dimension to the prose that can absorb a reader in the sheer beauty of the language. How does the language complement the fantastical elements in the novel?

   Look for powerful similes such as the one used to describe Eva's determination to ironically "save" Plum by killing him, when she goes "swooping like a giant heron" down the stairs (46). You could also discuss how many bizarre events are foreshadowed and described: for example, Eva "didn't willingly set foot on the stairs but once and that was to light a fire, the smoke of which was in her hair for years" (37).

2. **Imagery:** Vivid images enable readers to enter into the world that is created by the author. How do the images allow us to interpret the events that occur in Medallion?

   You may want to turn to the haunting images of various tragedies, such as Chicken Little's disappearance into the river, Eva's flight out of the window to extinguish the flames that are engulfing her daughter Hannah, and Sula and Jude engaged in the sex act. You could contrast these with calming images, such as the butterflies Ajax releases into Sula's house, and the deweys' beautiful teeth. Show how the images help to create the reader's idea of the town.

3. **African-American vernacular and naming:** How do the language in the text and the unusual names of people and places give us a rich sense of African-American culture?

Research into African-American vernacular could enhance your essay, or you could just limit yourself to the novel's rich examples of language. The ironic names could be a beginning point for an essay: you could examine the Peace family, who are far from experiencing tranquility, Tar Baby who is supposedly white and is named by a devious Eva, the Bottom, which paradoxically becomes coveted land that the whites end up moving into in the hills, and Ajax, who is named after a Greek god who was a hero in the Trojan war, but is stripped of his greatness when Sula finds out his name is Albert Jacks.

Compare and Contrast Essays

The book presents us with stark contrasts—contrasts that would make for a fascinating essay if explored in earnest. The pitfall to avoid is reducing your essay into a simplistic list of similarities and differences. You can avoid this mistake if you keep your focus on the complexities of certain relationships between opposite individuals or opposing forces. Try to find subtle pairs to compare and contrast, like the deweys and Tar Baby—first identify what they could possibly have as a basis of comparison. Both are abandoned, ridiculed, or simply ignored by society. Both appear mysteriously, without any true sense of self or of their heritage. They are also both objects of ridicule in a sense (with their strange names for starters), but are admired for uncanny traits—the deweys for their beautiful teeth, Tar Baby for his beautiful singing voice. After identifying similarities or differences, examine the characters' roles in the novel and what they represent to the Bottom's residents.

Sample Topics:

1. **Tar Baby versus Shadrack:** How do Tar Baby and Shadrack cope with their social ostracism?

These two lone figures may not appear to have any similarities. That is the beauty of *Sula*—the many subtle and unexpected connections between characters. Your essay could focus on who is more successful at survival. Although Tar Baby seems to be more a part of the community—engaging in social activities such as singing in the choir—he may be more of a tragic figure than Shadrack. Whose life is more meaningful in the community's eyes?

2. **Nel Wright and her mother, Helene, in contrast to Sula Mae Peace and her mother, Hannah:** Contrast Nel's relationship to her mother and Sula's interaction with her mother.

You could look at the ways both mothers introduce their daughters into a world of self-love or self-hatred, their attitudes toward sex, their expectations of them as women, and how these relationships affect them as adults. How do their relationships with their mothers influence their relationships with men and each other? How does Nel contend with her mother's over-protective molly-coddling, and how does Sula react to her mother's quiet disdain?

3. **Sula Mae Peace versus Nel Wright:** Nel and Sula's relationship is mystical and passionate: they met "in the delirium of their noon dreams" (51) and are described as inhabiting one body and mind. How do they converge and diverge as soul mates and friends?

There are many ways to contrast these two major characters. You could contrast their physical attributes: Sula's birthmark is described as a rose, a frightful black mark, a snake over her eye, a tadpole, and Hannah's ashes, depending on the spectator. Nel's looks are seldom mentioned apart from in contrast to her mother, who is glad she is not a beauty. But in an essay you need to go further than just identifying physical differences. How do these differences play a role in others' perceptions of them? Why does Nel allow her parents to strip her of any internal spark, whereas Sula argues with her grandmother that she'll "split this town in two . . . before I'll let you put it out" (93)?

4. **Compare imperfection in *Sula* and *Beloved*:** How does imperfection, physical or otherwise, play a role in characters' lives in these two novels?

Physical imperfection is a theme that can be found throughout Morrison's work, so you need not restrict yourself to these two novels. *Sula* and *Beloved* provide an interesting starting point because the examples of physical imperfections are so obvious—Sethe's scarred back and Eva's missing leg, for example. You might want to begin with various characters' self-image or understanding of their difference and examine whether they feel an emotional or physical loss. In *Sula*, Eva Peace returns to Medallion with only one leg but refuses to tell the curious townspeople what happened. Her strength and physical abilities are not diminished, and culminate in her heroic acts to save her son and daughter from physical and emotional death. In *Beloved* many characters feel emotional imperfection, or sense that something is missing in their lives. How does the physical or emotional disability play a role in character development, or the way the characters assess themselves?

Bibliography for *Sula*

Bergenholtz, Rita A. "Toni Morrison's Sula: A Satire on Binary Thinking." *African American Review* 30, no. 1 (1996): 89–98.

Bloom, Harold, ed. *Toni Morrison's* Sula. Bloom's Modern Critical Interpretations. Philadelphia: Chelsea House, 1999.

Galehouse, Maggie. "'New World Woman': Toni Morrison's *Sula*." *Papers on Language and Literature* 30, no. 4 (1999): 339–62.

Gates, Henry Louis, Jr., and K. A. Appiah, eds. *Toni Morrison: Critical Perspectives Past and Present.* Amistad Literary Series. New York: Amistad P, 1993.

Iyasere, Solomon O., and Marla W. Iyasere, eds. *Understanding Toni Morrison's* Beloved *and* Sula: *Selected Essays and Criticisms of the Works by the Nobel Prize–Winning Author.* New York: Whitston Publishing, 2000.

Lee, Rachel. "Missing Peace in Toni Morrison's *Sula* and *Beloved*." *African American Review* 28, no. 4 (1994): 571–83.

McDowell, Deborah. "'The Self and the Other': Reading Toni Morrison's *Sula* and the Black Female Text." In *Toni Morrison's* Sula. Bloom's Modern Critical Interpretations, edited by Harold Bloom, 149–63. New York: Chelsea House, 1990.

McKay, Nellie Y. *Critical Essays on Toni Morrison.* Boston: G. K. Hall, 1988.

SONG OF SOLOMON

READING TO WRITE

WRITING ABOUT *Song of Solomon*'s rich narrative can be a deeply satisfying and intriguing experience; the layers of narrative that occur alongside one man's quest for belonging leave the reader with many avenues to take when writing about the novel. One place to begin as a writer is with the epigraphs of the novel. The first epigraph is simply "Daddy," while the second acknowledges: "The fathers may soar/ And the children may know their names." Using these two epigraphs as entry points into the novel, one can begin to formulate ideas for an essay on the significance of names, identity, belonging, and the importance of family connections, all of which are central to the realities of many of the characters in the book.

In a fascinating scene in which Macon "Milkman" Dead III and Guitar Bains argue about their approaches to life, class-consciousness, and racism, among other issues, Guitar vehemently criticizes some of Milkman's life choices. Later on, Milkman considers Guitar's criticisms and reflects on his life purpose. A close reading of Milkman's internal musings can help lead us into an exploration of many different topics for an essay, based on the epigraphs that frame the action of the novel.

> If he had to spend the rest of his life thinking about rents and property, he'd lose his mind. But he was going to spend the rest of his life doing just that, wasn't he. That's what his father assumed and he supposed that was what he had assumed as well.
>
> Maybe Guitar was right—partly. His life was pointless, aimless. And it was true that he didn't concern himself an awful lot about other people.

There was nothing he wanted bad enough to risk anything for, inconvenience himself for. . . .

　　He ought to get married, Milkman thought. . . . Get a nice house. His father would help him find one. . . . And what? There had to be something better to look forward to. . . . He was bored. Everybody bored him. The city was boring. (107)

　　This scene is a wonderful one to explore further and is rich with potential essay choices, all of which can be directly related to the two epigraphs mentioned earlier. Milkman's malaise could be related to his lack of self-knowledge. The codependent and oppressive relationship between father and son is unmistakable. Milkman fails to realize the choke hold his father has had on his life and on his ability to make life-altering decisions. Both of them simply go along with the status quo—Macon Jr. making money, and Milkman following his example, simply because he does not have the creativity to view his life in any other way, even though if he continued that way, "he'd lose his mind." An essay could consider this life choice by examining Milkman's unease and certainty that "[t]here had to be something better to look forward to." A writer could relate Milkman's predicament to other characters who seem to be stuck in inertia, not able to improve their lives.

　　The epigraph suggests that knowledge of one's name is crucial to one's sense of well-being and self-actualization, and the quotation reveals that at that moment, Milkman knows neither the significance of his own and his father's and grandfather's name nor their legacy and his heritage. Years before, when Milkman was seventeen and came to his mother's defense by hitting his father, not only did Milkman not know the origin of his name (which leads to the discovery of his mother's inappropriate behavior with him), but he was ignorant about the relationship his mother and father shared, and his father's efforts to have his wife abort Milkman. The secrets that Milkman has to uncover could provide material for many possible essays. Most of the characters have secrets, and these could be identified in an essay and examined in light of the character's self-awareness.

　　Inherent in this quotation is Milkman's dissatisfaction with his "pointless, aimless" life. He is willing to marry someone just because society expects that of him, without a second thought to Hagar, his first cousin, who literally dies from a broken heart because he does not reciprocate her love. He lacks passion for love and life, and wants to continue living his life unconcerned for others' well-being, and settling for a "nice" house. His insipid life that is devoid of passion could be contrasted to his ironic quest for the gold; he ends up caring for people, being more than concerned for others, and passionately unearthing his family history.

The above passage focuses on Milkman's life, but the themes inherent in the passage could be applied to other characters in the novel. Who else in *Song of Solomon* is dissatisfied, going along with the status quo, not challenging their oppressors, and just surviving, rather than living passionately? Who in the novel is the antithesis to this detached way of life? The passage that we focused on also contains many of the novel's themes and philosophical issues that could be elaborated on in an essay: the search for identity, people's preoccupation with social status, finding one's purpose in life, taking risks, following in your parents' footsteps, and so on. The novel's multifaceted characters and multiple themes can be explored in detail to create interesting and thought-provoking essays.

TOPICS AND STRATEGIES

Here you will find a variety of topics to consider. It is up to you to interpret the events and characters in the novel in an original way. Doing your own research can help you to put some of the occurrences in the novel into historical context, and can also help you to identify a unique angle to the novel to address in your paper.

Themes

The supernatural, freedom, literal and figurative flying, the healing and destructive power of love—these are some of the themes that could be explored in thematic essays about *Song of Solomon*. Because many of the themes are closely linked to character development, you could blend a study of a theme with a study of one or more characters to produce a multifaceted essay. Try to identify what the characters' behaviors tell us about that particular theme, and what the theme may be telling us about the human condition. For example, how do Guitar's complicated relationship with Milkman and his membership in the Seven Days tell us about loyalty and betrayal?

Sample Topics:

1. **The search for identity:** Milkman's search for a sense of self can be analyzed by taking into account the many levels of identity that he struggles with. Describe some aspects of his identity that he uncovers and that he comes to terms with on his journey.

   Focusing on identity in the novel could lead to a basic summary of the novel, which you would want to avoid doing in a literary analysis paper. Instead, you could isolate aspects of Milkman's personality that are presented as character flaws, or realities of which he is unaware. For instance, you may consider his waking dreams. Milkman was born with a caul, which according to folklore, allows a child to see ghosts and inexplicable events. Does he utilize these visions to improve his life? What does he learn about himself through these visions?

2. **Success and failure:** In what ways are characters concerned with their success and failure?

   Writing about people's success and failure in the novel could involve questioning who is responsible for the character's sense of self. Not only do people's character traits play a role in their success, but society and other people can be responsible. First Corinthians Dead, for example, feels ashamed of her job as Michael-Mary Graham's maid, and is limited to that position solely because of her race. Her situation could be contrasted to her father's fight against his limitations and his determination to succeed financially in spite of the blockades erected by society to stop him from succeeding. Integral to a discussion on success in the novel are class-consciousness and status, both of which often involve race. Of course, in any Morrison novel, typical thematic notions such as success and failure are going to be complicated. How are definitions of success skewed when one examines the philosophy of the Seven Days men?

3. **The healing and destructive power of love:** Verses 6 and 7 of chapter 8 of the biblical book Song of Solomon state: "[F]or love is strong as death; jealousy is cruel as the grave: the coals

thereof are coals of fire, which hath a most vehement flame. Many waters cannot quench love" (KJV). How can you apply these biblical verses to characters' behavior in the novel?

For an essay on love, you could first read the biblical book Song of Solomon and then relate the verses to various characters' experiences with love. Examine how people's views of love and their actions are integral to the action of the novel. Hagar's love is compared to an "anaconda," (137), and she becomes quite "vehement" as the biblical verse states, in contrast to Milkman's indifference. What light does knowledge of the biblical verses shed on the unfolding of events?

Character

Dynamic characters are those who undergo some sort of permanent change by the end of the novel, whether the change is apparent in their behavior or because of some acquired knowledge. All of the characters, even minor ones, undergo a transformation, which is one of the major themes in the novel. For an essay on character, you could explore how these characters change and whether the change is convincing. You could also identify the catalyst that brings about the change, and if the change is at anybody else's expense. Rather than present a list of characteristics or behaviors, link the personality trait to a theme or philosophical idea so that your essay explores a number of aspects of the novel, rather than simply a person's disposition.

Sample Topics:

1. **Ruth Foster Dead's character:** What motivates Ruth, and does she show evidence of transformation?

   In the Bible, Ruth is loyal, steadfast and devoted. In *Song of Solomon,* Ruth has all of these qualities, but instead of exhibiting love for a mother-in-law (which has been interpreted as lesbian love in the Bible), Ruth shows this devotion for her father. Macon interprets her love for her father as unnatural, and Milkman learns of the incestuous relationship through a conversation with his father. Why does Morrison allow us to see Ruth's conflicting side of the story? How can you relate the two versions of the story to the form of the novel—and the ways various characters get their chances to tell their stories, but at different times?

2. **Pilate Dead's character:** How do Pilate's characteristics function in contrast to other characters in the novel?

   Pilate's complicated character could be explored in an essay in contrast to other characters. Pilate and her brother, Macon Dead, cold be contrasted, as could Pilate and her niece First Corinthians. What commentary is Morrison making by presenting us with African-American women who are confined by society (like Corinthians) and those who live completely on the outskirts of society's rigid norms (like Pilate)? You could relate this juxtaposition to Milkman's thoughts of Pilate in terms of "her ugliness, her poverty, her dirt, and her wine" (38), and later as the story of her life is revealed to him, the fact that he changes his harsh and dogmatic view of her.

3. **Guitar Bains's character:** What drives Guitar, and how does he become an antagonistic force in the novel?

   Guitar is another character who could automatically be compared to others in the novel, and, of course, principally as a foil to Milkman. When writing about the two, though, avoid simplistic reductions of their characters to good and evil. Morrison's depiction of the friends defies a simplistic interpretation, because their interactions are so complicated and both exhibit admirable and reprehensible character traits. How does Guitar develop as a character? In what way is Guitar a spokesperson for the frustrations that many African Americans were burdened with during this historical period? Why does Guitar turn against Milkman at the end of the novel?

4. **First Corinthians Dead's Character:** How is First Corinthians developed as a sympathetic character?

Morrison's clever naming of characters adds to the complexity of this sensitive character. You could look up the biblical verse and see how her character reflects some of the lessons from the Bible, and what personality traits endear her to the reader. The situation First Corinthians finds herself in and the emotions she experiences are echoed in other novels in characters whose potential is squashed by a racist and sexist society. Her longing for a better life is shared by the reader, and we want her to succeed in becoming "a grown-up woman that's not scared of her daddy" (196) as Porter puts it. You could also include the effect that her brother Milkman and her sister Lena have on her search for autonomy.

History and Context

Morrison alludes to many historical events in the novel. You could pinpoint some of these and do further research into them. Overall, the characters live in a society that requires social change, social justice, and a reprieve from racial violence. For example, Emmett Till's gruesome murder, which is referred to in the novel, illustrates the violence that many African-American men faced in the 1950s. The characters who make up the Seven Days answer this violent reality by creating a threat of their own. What does the novel say about revenge, calculated violence, and passivity?

Sample Topics:

1. **Land allocation:** Identify the importance of land in the novel.

   There are many examples of the importance of the land. Macon Dead Senior is murdered because of the land that he owned. In an essay on such a topic, you may want to research sharecropping and the allocation of land to slaves and freedmen during and after slavery to get a sense of the significance of land. Another approach to a study of the land could be the way the land features in a poetic and visual way during Guitar's chase of Milkman when the group of men goes hunting; the chase through the forest is a memorable scene that is full of anxiety and fast-paced suspense.

2. **Racial violence:** How does the violence in the novel serve as a backdrop for the historical time period and frame the characters' realities?

There are many types of violence—racial and otherwise—that you could discuss at length in an essay. The novel opens with self-inflicted violence, the suicide of Mr. Smith, the insurance agent, which could be representative of the plight of the average African-American man at the time. His ability to thrive in the world is perhaps limited by his race. The reader later finds out the reason for his apparently inexplicable suicide. Avoid just listing instances of violence; instead tie them to character, theme, or language. For example, Mr. Smith's suicide is linked to flight and freedom, and later on, once the truth comes out (another theme), his death is connected to racial hostility. Various characters also have flashbacks of his suicide throughout the book, so you could connect their responses and the poetic language used to describe the death to the characters' memories.

3. **Songs in African-American literature and folklore:** How do literal and figurative song add to the narrative?

Song has been an important part of African-American creative expression, and this reality shows up in the literature. Many African-American expressions of liberation from oppression have come in the form of song, so it is no surprise, since this book has freedom as a key thematic idea, that song would feature prominently. How do the songs that Milkman hears help him solve the mystery of his ancestry?

Philosophy and Ideas

This novel encourages contemplation about a number of issues that poets, playwrights, philosophers, and religious figures have pondered for centuries. You may want to examine the way the book reflects upon revenge killing and all of the moral implications contained therein. Interestingly,

Milkman's character deliberately tries *not* to think too much about his predicament and would rather go along with the status quo. In contrast, Macon Dead thinks too much about money, and when Porter is on the verge of suicide, all he can think about is getting back the money that Porter owes him. An essay on philosophical ideas could be fascinating since there are so many issues to choose from.

Sample Topics:

1. **Memory, and people's relationship to it:** Explore the role of memory in the novel.

   A starting point for an essay on the intricacies of memory could be the part in the novel when Macon Dead tells his son Milkman, "Funny how things get away from you. For years you can't remember nothing. Then just like that, it all comes back to you" (52). Milkman's quest allows him to unearth the history that Pilate and Macon are ignorant of, when he is exposed to the collective memory of the old men in Shalimar. You could examine why so many characters block out the past or distort the past. Is it a deliberate attempt to obscure what really happened, or is it a survival skill? People's distortion of the past and their selective memory is closely linked to the truth, and differing perceptions of the truth, as discussed below.

2. **The "whole truth":** Why does Macon Dead tell his son Milkman that it is imperative to know the "whole truth" rather than just one person's story? Who else knows only partial truths, or half of the story?

   To address these ideas in an essay, you could look at the prevalence of secrets that people harbor in the novel and how the secrets affect people's sense of trust and identity. Some characters deliberately keep secrets from others. What are some of the reasons for these secret lives? Ruth tells Milkman, "I know, as well as I know my own name, that [Macon] told you only what was flattering to him" (124), and this revelation allows him to believe yet more of his father's perspective. Guitar and

Milkman share a deep friendship and are aware that they both have secrets that they are keeping from each other. How does Morrison share some of the secrets with the reader and carefully reveal them to the characters involved?

3. **Literal and figurative death:** What roles do literal and figurative deaths play in the lives of characters?

The men in Milkman's family often point out that because their last name is Dead, they already are dead. In what ways are the male family members figuratively dead? Other characters fear figurative deaths, for example Ruth Foster is scared that she will die in a marriage with no intimacy (125). The irony present in the book is also that in order to figuratively and literally live, many characters have to "kill" an unhelpful or menacing aspect of their personalities. Guitar has to leave behind his compassion for others in order to survive as the Sunday man, for example.

Form and Genre

One way to analyze Morrison's work is by assessing the way the author crafts the novel. The form of *Song of Solomon* has been described as "epic quest." In addition, *Song of Solomon* incorporates many aspects of other types of literature, such the myth of the slaves who flew back to Africa to escape slavery, a common theme in African-American folklore. The use of literary devices such as irony and mystery are also prevalent in the book. The shift in setting from the city to the countryside also plays a role in characters' sentiments and behavior. Morrison allows us to see different perspectives regarding a situation, such as Milkman's indifference to Hagar and her emotional response to him. How is the novel shaped by the many voices relating their stories?

Sample Topics:

1. **The protagonist's epic quest:** The novel is separated into two parts: Milkman's and other characters' lives before his quest in part one, and then the quest and its aftermath in part two.

How does the quest transform the protagonist and other characters?

Writing about Milkman's figurative and literal journey could evoke comparisons to other archetypal heroes' quests. Inherent within Milkman's quest is a quest for self-improvement. At first, he is not sure what really needs to change in his life: All he cares about is finding the gold and improving his life financially, even though money bores him. As his quest progresses, he becomes more and more invested in actually finding out his history, and the gold is of secondary importance. Milkman's physical journey, like that of many literary heroes, includes a figurative and literal baptism and cleansing when he slips in the river and is completely submerged under the water. He battles the natural landscape but emerges reborn.

2. **Dramatic irony and irony of situation:** How do dramatic irony and irony of situation work in the novel?

Dramatic irony occurs when a character is unaware of the significance of his or her actions, behaviors, or thoughts, but the reader can clearly see the reality. Irony of situation occurs when a character ends up in an unexpected situation, or one that is the direct opposite from how they started in the beginning of the novel. An essay could look at the irony of situation that occurs with Hagar's death. It is ironic that while Milkman is experiencing a rebirth, Hagar is dying of a broken heart. Exploring the various characters' lives allows a writer to look at the depiction of life's ironies.

3. **Mystery:** How does mystery work in the novel?

Irony and mystery seem to work together in the book, in most of the characters' lives and in the thematic content. Inherent in characters' ignorance and quest for knowledge is, of course, a mystery to be solved or a secret that has to be revealed.

Milkman's quest begins with the mystery of the gold and ends with the mystery of his identity. He solves the latter, and the former mystery pales into insignificance. A writer could examine how much knowledge and insight the reader acquires and how the characters' lack of knowledge affects the reader.

Language, Symbols, and Imagery

The language in the novel provides many opportunities for a writer to explore its richness in an essay. The conversations people engage in are witty and full of insights into life and human suffering and joy. The depth of human feelings is conveyed to us through people's language and also through their silence. Sometimes language cannot express how a person feels, as with Corinthians's figurative near-death experience. If she loses Porter, she feels she will truly die. She cannot convey that in words, so she says nothing and instead climbs onto his car and lies prostrate, full of emotion and fear. In an exploration of language, you could also comment on its failure to convey feelings.

Sample Topics:

1. **Figurative language: allusions:** Allusions to the Bible abound in the novel. What role does the biblical Song of Solomon play in the novel?

   The biblical Song of Solomon echoes many of the characters' states of mind in the novel. Chapter 2 verse 5 seems to tell us Milkman's feelings: "I am sick of love", and in contrast, chapter 3 verse 4 could be interpreted as Corinthians's feelings: "I found him whom my soul loveth: I held him, and would not let him go." Chapter 5 verse 6 could echo Hagar's feelings about Milkman: "I opened to my beloved; but my beloved had withdrawn himself, and was gone" (KJV). You could familiarize yourself with the biblical verses and then explore characters who seem to act in the way the verse suggests.

2. **Imagery:** Sensory perception features widely in the novel. Explore the importance of smell in the novel, and its connection to character development.

Writing on the sense of smell in the novel could uncover connections with a character, a theme, or language, for example. References to smell can be found in the biblical book Song of Solomon and can be connected to characters and their confusion or lack of awareness. For example, you could look at what Pilate's and Circe's smells represent. You could also analyze how Guitar Bains's sensory memory of sweets invokes his father's gruesome death and how the subsequent psychic pain follows him into adulthood. How is sensory perception used to illuminate life experiences?

3. **African-American vernacular and naming:** How are names and the act of naming used in the context of a society that is hostile to African Americans?

The names in the novel are curious and often have humorous connotations. Rather than provide a list of the obscure names in the book, you might contemplate names in relation to historical occurrences. Slave codes prohibited the enslaved from being taught how to read or write. Later on, African Americans were prohibited from voting unless they could spell their names. You could connect these historical realities to the names of characters in the book, such as that of Macon Dead. Macon Dead's mother approved of her husband's spurious new name, because as Macon says, she thought that a new name could "wipe out the past" (54). How is naming at the root of a lot of identity confusion in the novel? How is naming liberating?

Bibliography for *Song of Soloman*

Campbell, Joseph. *The Hero with a Thousand Faces.* Princeton, NJ: Princeton UP, 1973.

Duvall, John N. *The Identifying Fictions of Toni Morrison: Modernist Authenticity and Postmodern Blackness.* New York: Palgrave, 2000.

Gates, Henry Louis, Jr., and K. A. Appiah, eds. *Toni Morrison: Critical Perspectives Past and Present.* Amistad Literary Series. New York: Amistad P, 1993.

Mbalia, Doreatha Drummond. *Toni Morrison's Developing Class Consciousness.* Selinsgrove, PA: Susquehanna UP, 2004.

McKay, Nellie Y. *Critical Essays on Toni Morrison.* Boston: G. K. Hall, 1988.

O'Reilly, Andrea. *Toni Morrison and Motherhood: A Politics of the Heart.* New York: State U of New York P, 2004.

White, Shane, and Graham J. White. *The Sounds of Slavery: Discovering African American History Through Songs, Sermons, and Speech.* Boston, MA: Beacon P, 2005.

TAR BABY

READING TO WRITE

THE EPIGRAPH of *Tar Baby*, taken from First Corinthians in the Bible, states, ". . . there are/ contentions among you," and many of the relationships and events in the novel involve contention of some sort. The origin of the strife is varied but often relates to the historic interactions between whites and blacks, men and women, parents and children. Love is also at the core of this powerful novel, and both causes and soothes the conflicts that occur. Because of the narrative's multiple themes, philosophical ideas, myths, and historic backgrounds, *Tar Baby* offers many subjects to write about. A close reading of any section can uncover thematic concerns, character motivation and historical issues that you may want to explore in an essay.

In terms of the plot, contention and strife among the characters build slowly and climax at the Christmas dinner at Valerian Street's home. Everyone's frustrations surface, along with personality traits and secrets that had remained hidden:

> "Whatever mischief I did," [William "Son" Green] said, "it wasn't enough to make you leave the table to find out about it."
>
> "You will leave this house," said Valerian. "Now."
>
> "I don't think so," said Son. . . .
>
> Jadine spoke. "Valerian, Ondine's feelings were hurt. That's all."
>
> "By what, pray? By my removing a pair of thieves from my house?"
>
> "No, by not telling her," said Margaret.
>
> "So what? All of a sudden I'm beholden to a cook for the welfare of two people she hated anyway?" . . .

> "Mr. Street," said Sydney, "my wife is as important to me as yours is to you and should have the same respect."
>
> "More," said Ondine. "I should have more respect. I am the one who cleans up her shit!"
>
> "Ondine!" Both Sydney and Valerian spoke at once.
>
> "This is impossible!" Valerian was shouting. (206–07)

This heated exchange involves all of the major characters and many of the major philosophical themes in the novel. Valerian, the white upper-class landowner who is representative of the archetypal slave master, struggles for control of his workers and fires Gideon and Marie-Therese Foucault for stealing some apples, to the horror of Sydney and Ondine. In this passage Valerian calls Sydney and Ondine's loyalty and honesty into question, and it becomes apparent that Valerian does not view them with as much esteem as they had imagined. You could investigate the interactions between Valerian and those over whom he has financial control and write an interesting essay about dominance and submissiveness in relation to characters' perceptions of racial and financial superiority.

William "Son" Green's behavior in this passage can be linked to his character development. At the beginning of the novel, Son infiltrates the family by hiding in the bedrooms and stealing chocolate. He is filthy, starving, and barely surviving off the chocolate and water that Therese allows him to take. As the novel progresses, he goes from having animalistic characteristics to expressing deeply insightful perceptions about life.

Other philosophical ideas abound in this section, and can be examined in essays, such as people's complicity in situations where others compromise themselves morally—for example, Ondine's years of silence about Margaret's abuse of Michael. The role of power in relationships, such as the master/slave dichotomy, and gender interactions could also be examined. In this scene, Jadine does not defend her uncle and aunt. By keeping silent, does she tacitly endorse Valerian's behavior? She is indebted to Valerian, but at the same time she is aware of his control over her, so she does not dare to challenge his authority. Do the author or reader judge Jadine?

The novel additionally seems to comment on the way history impacts present-day life. An essay examining the repercussions of slavery and how it produced class and race stratification could be interesting, since so much of the novel's action includes references to class difference. On the micro-level, certain characters' histories could be analyzed and also the ways their upbringing affects their current lives.

TOPICS AND STRATEGIES

Here you will find a variety of topics to consider. It is up to you to interpret the events and characters in the novel in an original way. Doing your own research can help you to put some of the occurrences in the novel into historical context, and can also help you to identify your own unique approach to the novel.

Themes

The subject matter, ideas, and concepts that the story focuses on can be examined in relation to what these ideas seem to be telling us about the human condition. In *Tar Baby,* people experience love and the passion and the desire that go along with it. People also experience profound amounts of doubt and suffering in their daily lives. When you identify a theme that you would like to explore further, try to see if Morrison is making a commentary about it, or asking us to think critically or empathetically about that particular kind of human behavior.

Sample Topics:

1. **Food:** What role does the consumption and/or preparation of food play in some of the characters' lives?

   Including character development or some thematic elements may help to make a discussion of food more meaningful. Valerian and Margaret often focus on food. At the beginning of the novel they focus on the calories in a dish; later, we see the many connotations they assign to food—how it helps to assuage Margaret's guilt. Food also becomes an object of desire, when Therese and Gideon steal apples and Valerian fires them. Sydney and Ondine's servitude revolves around food and the food items that Margaret desires so that she can create a traditional turkey dinner for Christmas. What does food mean, in terms of characters' economic or political status?

2. **Parenting:** How does parenting manifest itself in the novel?

There are many types of relationships that recreate the parent-child dichotomy, so you may not have to limit yourself to traditional parents and children in an essay on this topic (see Love below, and the slave/master dichotomy discussed in Philosophy and Ideas). Valerian Street claims that Margaret has effectively destroyed Michael's chances of being a contributing member of society and that Margaret manipulates Michael to get attention then loses interest in him. Valerian's criticisms of her suffocating mothering come before he finds out her terrible secret. Jadine and Ondine also have an interesting guardian-child relationship that could be explored. The expectations that are inherent within these relationships will add another dimension to your discussion, as will people's desires to belong, give and receive forgiveness, and experience true love.

3. **Love:** Write about the different forms of love in the novel.

You could compare and contrast various manifestations of love, or focus on two people and their love for each other. What is interesting about the complicated expressions of love in the book is that they often intersect with class, race, identity, and other social issues. Jadine Childs and William "Son" Green share love that is committed, all-encompassing, and in some cases, like a parent-child relationship because their bond causes Jadine to feel that "[h]e unorphaned her completely" (229). Their love is also fraught with conflicts, such as his desire to remain on the outskirts of modern society and what he sees are its trappings, and her desire for him to conform to society's norms in order to achieve success.

4. **Self-Image:** What role does self-image play in characters' lives?

The contrast between the way people perceive themselves and the way others perceive them is central to Morrison's work.

Often the reader is privy to information that a character is not, creating dramatic irony:We have knowledge about a character that the character does not have. Sometimes the discrepancy in perception can be caused by other characters reacting with prejudice to that character's race or class. On occasion in *Tar Baby* we can see a character such as Jadine Childs respond to the way others perceive her, and these moments could be expounded on in an essay. Who in the novel seems to be defined by their position in society? Does anyone transcend the expected societal roles? What role do initial appearances play in the novel?

Character

Below, multiple characters are presented as units; you may want to think about Sydney and Ondine Childs as a single character, for example. This is just a suggestion, since the characters could also be analyzed separately. Strongly tied to characterization are history and folklore: The slave history that Morrison explores, and the African-American folklore that she incorporates in the narrative. Some of the characters seem to be recreating historical roles, like the master/slave roles that society sanctioned and prescribed and that people could not escape at that historical moment. Is Morrison claiming that these roles or archetypes are an inevitable result of modern life and human interactions?

Sample Topics:

1. **Sydney and Ondine Childs as a character:** Are Sydney and Ondine Childs passive victims of their life circumstance? How does their role change during the course of the novel?

   After examining the husband and wife couple, you might contrast them as a unit to the marital unit of Margaret and Valerian Street. The descriptions of Sydney's precision and dedication are fascinating, as is Ondine's sense of ownership of the kitchen. What causes some of the disagreements between him and Ondine? What makes them both finally lose their composure?

2. **Margaret and Valerian Street as a character:** How do Margaret and Valerian Street function in the novel?

Margaret Street's internal conflict revolves around her guilty secret of mistreating her son, Michael, when he was a baby. The symptoms of this guilt present themselves in the form of dementia, when she, for example, confuses objects and lives in fear of making a mistake. Valerian Street often closely monitors what she eats, and ridicules her actions. She tells him, "You make everything I do sound stupid" (66). The relationship is riddled with disagreements stemming from his sense that she is drinking, his superiority, and her remorse. Her identity is indistinguishable from her role of mother and wife, so analyzing Valerian and Margaret as a unit is an interesting option.

3. **The island and New York (the setting) as characters:** How does the personification of New York and Isle des Chevaliers allow the setting to be a character?

Analyzing the setting as if it were a character could yield a thought-provoking discussion. The setting often comes alive in the book, and influences characters' actions and thoughts. You may look at the connections that characters have to their surroundings and what effect the landscape has on the characters. For example, Jadine thinks to herself, "The island exaggerated everything. . . . Such tranquility in sleep made for wildness during the waking hours" (68); then while in New York, Son feels the sadness of people around him and has difficulty adjusting to life there.

History and Context

Putting *Tar Baby* into historical context deepens one's comprehension of the novel. For example, having some background in Caribbean history and colonization would help when writing an essay on the island as a character. Colonization of the islands by the French (in this fictional case) created a system of class and race stratification that privileged a few locals but disadvantaged many. You can use history to help you augment an essay on certain characters and their behaviors. Caribbean history is fraught with contention, which is one of the major thematic ideas in the novel, and much of this contention came about because of the kind of social inequality illustrated in *Tar Baby*.

Sample Topics:

1. **Slavery's legacy:** How does Morrison present us with a modern culture that remains impacted by the legacy of slavery?

   The characters in the novel could be said to be suffering from the psychic wounds of slavery. Son tells Jadine that black and white people should simply not interact. What is Morrison telling us about the ways historical tragedies resonate hundreds of years later? When Son returns to his ancestors, so to speak, by going to find the blind horsemen, what is Morrison's point? Is she implying that healing from this kind of historical pain can come about only through sacrifice?

2. **The historical importance of the family in African-American culture:** How is the family as a social unit redefined by the characters in *Tar Baby*?

   Son's desire to visit his family in the all-black town of Eloe could provide interesting material for an essay. Jadine's resistance to the place and her defiance of expected respectful behavior create a major conflict in the couple's relationship. Jadine is also terribly bored there and mocks Son's history and legacy. When her pictures are developed, it is interesting to note that she feels that his family members look ridiculous in the photos. Ironically, although Jadine has no real family, she does not want to accept Son's as her own. An essay could look at Jadine's family, or lack thereof, and how she practically abandons her only family members, Sydney and Ondine, at the end of the novel.

3. **Physical appearance and color-consciousness:** How are characters limited by their physical appearance and the ways others view them because of their race?

Alma Estes's partiality to wigs can be explored in an essay, along with perhaps another aspect of the novel that deals with people's sense of self. Her desire to get new wigs from America can be interpreted with a historical lens and as an act of self-hatred—the act of covering up her hair with fake hair to appear more European. This act could be related to Jadine's love of the seal fur coat and the way Son thinks about the way the natural world has been destroyed and depleted by mankind's new technologies.

Philosophy and Ideas

Because so much of the novel consists of peoples' internal monologues, there is no shortage of philosophical issues to explore in an essay. Any character's stream of consciousness could provide substantial material to ponder, especially since the characters wonder about race, class, their sense of belonging, and their guilt formed by keeping secrets—major issues that most people struggle with. Inherent within their mindful musings are issues of the human condition. At times the characters struggle with their life purpose and the role society has placed them in, and whether they should fight that or support the status quo. Does everyone in the novel possess such self-awareness and clarity? What effect does the lack of self-knowledge have on characters and their outcome?

Sample Topics:

1. **Self-actualization:** In what ways are the acts of self-actualization and self-definition important in the lives of the characters?

In approaching an essay on self-actualization and self-definition, think about Abraham Maslow's hierarchy of needs and the definition of a self-actualized person as one who transcends cultural entrapment and is self-accepting, powerful, and living his true purpose. Son seems to go up the hierarchy of needs during the course of the novel from survival, security, social acceptance, and self-esteem to self-actualization. Maslow's concepts can be applied within the context of the novel to naming or being named in a derogatory way by others, as well as to class differences, racial hostility, and love.

2. **Master/servant dichotomy:** What do the interactions between the Streets and the Childs illustrate about the master and servant relationship?

An interesting research project could come from a comparison of actual slave narratives, for example from those in *Voices from Slavery: 100 Authentic Slave Narratives* by Norman R. Yetman (1970), and this modern-day narrative of servitude in which the interactions between the Childs and the Streets often read like the novel is set during slavery. Sydney and Ondine Childs, who are literally dependents of Valerian Street, live a life in which "[e]ighty percent of [their] conversation was the caprice and habits of their master" (226).

3. **Physical/metaphorical cleansing:** How are characters transformed through either a physical or metaphorical cleansing?

An essay may discuss the scene when Jadine falls into the swamp and has to use turpentine to cleanse herself of the thick oil-like substance that almost fatally consumed her. Her ritual bathing and cleansing could be compared to Son's hunger, filth, and eventual transformation. Filth and purity can be examined in the literal and figurative ways that they show up in the book, along with what they seem to represent. Sydney refers to Son as a "swamp nigger" when he first appears, and everyone focuses on his terrible blackness and filth which seem to contribute to the perception of him as a physical and sexual threat. In Jadine's case, her entrapment in the swamp could symbolically mean that she is the tar baby from the tale, as discussed below.

Form and Genre

An analysis of the way that Morrison creates the novel can lead to interesting discussions. The genre is the type of work, in this case fiction, and the form is the structure of the work, in this case a story told with various narrative voices. Look for the many literary devices (such as allusions to the Bible) that the author uses to create and inform the narrative. What else shapes the novel? How do we get to see into many characters' minds, and what effect does this have on the reader?

Sample Topics:

1. **Narrative voice:** How do the narrative voice and stream of consciousness shape the novel?

   The diverse voices tell us the story from different perspectives and allow us into the worlds of people from different races, classes, ages, and backgrounds. The narrative allows for a shift in point of view from character to character that gives us many opportunities to analyze human shortcomings and human suffering. The three main couples are equally important to the action of the novel, and their lives are carefully woven together as the events unfold. Stream of consciousness could be written about as a tool that many authors implement to show us the inner musings of characters' minds at work. We see the random thoughts of almost every major character, and this helps the reader to understand their philosophical beliefs.

2. ***Tar Baby* as modern-day folklore:** How is the narrative linked to the folklore story of Brer Rabbit and the tar baby?

   Familiarizing yourself with the folklore story sheds light on the literary allusion. Son tells Jadine the story of the tar baby to mock her in one of their heated arguments, alluding to the fact that she is the tar baby that trapped Brer Rabbit (270). Interpreting Son as Brer Rabbit, the all-knowing trickster, and Jadine as the tar baby who is set by the fox to ensnare him, could create an interesting essay. Brer Rabbit, of course, escapes though his own cunning, and that ending could be contrasted to the novel's end, when Therese leads Son to his freedom with the legendary blind horsemen who roam the island.

3. *Tar Baby* **as social commentary:** In what ways does the novel comment on society? Would you say parts of the narrative are social satire?

There is a lot to write about on the novel as a satire, or ridicule, of certain aspects of society. Many of the characters themselves engage in bitter critiques of societal expectations. Son's and Valerian's attitudes, for example the heated conversation about stealing the apples (205), could be contrasted, particularly their views on ownership, oppression, and human rights. You could contrast what the two symbolize here—and maybe relate it to the legacy of slavery.

Language, Symbols, and Imagery

Morrison's use of language, symbols, and imagery in her fiction is the focus of much scrutiny. The language of her novels surprises, delights, and challenges the reader. The language in *Tar Baby* is complicated by the fact that the setting is a French Caribbean Island. The nuances of people's speech and misunderstandings caused by language barriers could be addressed in an essay. Morrison also shows how language has been used as a tool of oppression, and there are many examples of this in the book that you can identify and discuss. How do characters create a sense of self-importance and authority by the names they call others? The intellectual conversation that Jadine and Son engage in could be scrutinized in an essay, since it is the cause of much of the contention between them. Not only do people's words hold a lot of power, but in *Tar Baby* even the trees think and talk, or murmur to one another. Examples of figurative language abound, such as the personification of the landscape, and these instances can be explored in depth as long as the meaning behind the figurative language is explored.

Sample Topics:

1. **Personification:** How do examples of personification contribute to the development of the narrative?

Because there are so many inanimate objects and aspects of nature that are personified in the novel, you have a lot of material to work with if writing about this type of figurative language. What you may want to do is tie the instances of personification in with the narrative voice, or the tone of the novel. The waves, the moon, the fog—they are all given human characteristics. However, simply identifying and describing instances of personification is not enough. Connect the personification to the effect on particular characters or maybe the island as a character.

2. **Imagery:** Explore the use of visual imagery in *Tar Baby.*

The unmistakable setting of the novel can provide plenty of material for discussion in an essay on imagery. Not only is the setting remarkable, but the rich descriptions of characters could also be analyzed. Valerian's eyes, for example, are mentioned many times. You may pick a visual image and connect it to the behavior of a character or the expectations that others have of a character because of his or her physical attributes. The visuals in the novel could also be closely tied to figurative language, such as dramatic irony; for example, Margaret looks as though everything is fine, but inside she lives in fear that people will discover her secret.

3. **Naming:** How is naming used in the novel as a tool of empowerment or disempowerment?

Most of Morrison's novels creatively name characters and places. Writing about the names in this novel might include a discussion on the ways people name others without their knowledge. For example, Sydney and Jadine call Son "Nigger," and Therese calls Ondine "Machete head." Secret names could reveal attitudes about perceptions, but do they dehumanize a person who does not know about them? The secret names may also be ironic, so you could include a discussion of figurative language so that your essay is not one-dimensional.

Bibliography for *Tar Baby*

Gates, Henry Louis, Jr., and K. A. Appiah, eds. *Toni Morrison: Critical Perspectives Past and Present.* Amistad Literary Series. New York: Amistad P, 1993.

Harding, Wendy, and Jacky Martin. *A World of Difference: An Inter-Cultural Study of Toni Morrison's Novels.* Westport, CT: Greenwood P, 1994.

Maslow, Abraham. "A Theory of Human Motivation." *Psychological Review* 50 (1943): 370–96.

O'Reilly, Andrea. *Toni Morrison and Motherhood: A Politics of the Heart.* New York: State U of New York P, 2004.

Ryan, Judylyn S. "Contested Visions/Double-Vision in Tar Baby," *Modern Fiction Studies* 39, no. 3 (1993): 597–621.

Yetman, Norman R. *Voices from Slavery: 100 Authentic Slave Narratives.* New York: Dover Publications, 1970.

"RECITATIF"

READING TO WRITE

TONI MORRISON's only published short story, "Recitatif," first appeared in *Confirmation: An Anthology of African-American Women* edited by Amiri and Amina Baraka in 1983. The editor Amiri Baraka is an influential writer whose poetry and plays in the 1960s and later sparked intense debate about race relations in America and African Americans' role in their liberation from racial oppression. When "Recitatif" was first published, Morrison was a well-known author but had not yet written the Pulitzer prize–winning *Beloved*. "Recitatif" later appeared in *Leaving Home* in 1997, after Morrison had won the Nobel Prize in literature. This later anthology of short stories, based around the theme of home and belonging, was edited by Hazel Rochman and Darlene Z. McCampbell.

Analyzing the historical setting of the short story would be one way to write about it. Also, putting the story in the context of Morrison's other works helps in examining the themes in the story. At the time of publishing, Morrison had written *The Bluest Eye, Sula,* and *Tar Baby*. Keep that in mind when you write about the themes that she is well known for, since *Beloved, Jazz,* and *Paradise,* that examine the effects of slavery, were not yet written, but the themes of the aftereffects of slavery and injustice can be found in "Recitatif."

Doing a close reading of a text can help in writing about it, since you can identify major themes of the work, isolate their meaning, and put them into a larger historical context. The following passage from the short story reveals many of the themes that are apparent in the work:

Mary, simpleminded as ever, grinned and tried to yank her hand out of the pocket with the raggedy lining—to shake hands, I guess. Roberta's mother looked down at me and then looked down at Mary too. She didn't say anything, just grabbed Roberta with her Bible-free hand and stepped out of line, walking quickly to the rear of it. Mary was still grinning because she's not too swift when it comes to what's really going on. Then this light bulb goes off in her head and she says "That bitch!" really loud and us almost in the chapel now. . . . All I could think of was that she really needed to be killed. The sermon lasted a year, and I knew the real orphans were looking smug again. (7)

The irony of the mother and daughter swapping roles is apparent in this quotation. Earlier on, Twyla says her mother looks like she is the child waiting for her mother, not the other way around. This exchange in roles is an important part of the mother-daughter relationship, and illustrates the themes of belonging, abandonment, safety, and a loss of innocence. Twyla's innocence and juxtaposing wisdom are contrasted to her mother being "simpleminded as ever." In an essay, you could explore how Morrison imbues her eight-year-old narrator with authority, confidence, and intelligence in spite of her age and situation. How do we get a sense of Twyla's intelligence and maturity?

The passage above also illustrates the racial conflicts present in society when Roberta's mother refuses to shake Mary's hand. Because of the ambiguity of the race of the characters, it is unclear if the act of refusing to acknowledge the other comes from the black woman or the white woman. Morrison's point is probably that it is unimportant: The damage lies in the fact that people would disrespect one another because of race. Race is not the only source of conflict; the fact that the girls are abandoned by their mothers and forced to rely on each other to understand the world is another focal point of conflict. Examining the form of the piece could also provide for an interesting essay, given that Morrison is primarily a novelist.

TOPICS AND STRATEGIES

Here you will find a variety of topics to consider. It is up to you to interpret the events and characters in the story in an original way. Doing your own research can help you to situate some of the occurrences in the short story into historical context and can also help you to identify a unique approach to the story.

Themes

Writers can identify themes in a work of literature by paying attention to repeated or emphasized words, ideas, or patterns of behavior, since all of these may suggest themes or concepts in the short story. Once you have identified a theme, try to uncover what the story is saying about the theme. When writing about theme, you may write about connected themes, such as abandonment and fear, and you may find some of your themes blending with the Philosophies and Ideas suggestions that are explored in the later section. Themes in the story include but are not limited to racism, taking responsibility for one's actions, the innocence of youth, and parenting.

Sample Topics:

1. **Friendship:** How does the fact that the two girls, Twyla and Roberta, are left by their mothers play a role in their friendship?

   Writing about the friendship in the story would involve looking at the ways the connection between the two girls changes over time. How does the relationship evolve over the years?

2. **Shame:** How does shame play a role in the characters' lives?

   Writing about shame would probably involve a discussion of abandonment, since the two are closely connected for the girls who are left by their mothers in the shelter for orphans. Both girls seem to feel on the outside, even in a place where the other children are pitied by society, because they are not "real orphans."

Character

Writing about character could include a discussion of character traits, how the author shows us a character is a particular way, and the changes a character undergoes in the course of the short story. You can investigate what the characters' behaviors mean in that specific social context and how Morrison creates believable characters who are often unpredictable. In this story, the child narrator plays a role in shaping the reader's view of the other characters, and that reality could be addressed in an essay.

Sample Topics:

1. **The two mothers' characters:** How are the two mothers symbolic of racial tensions in America?

   The racial ambiguity of the protagonists is an interesting focus for an essay. Some clues are given, but the reader has to decide whether assigning a race to each is important, or whether the omission is the very point that Morrison may be making: that race is arbitrary.

2. **Roberta Fisk's character:** How are Roberta's actions accounted for?

   As a child, Roberta embraces Twyla, and they become a unit of strength, battling against the older girls and keeping at bay their sense of shame about being abandoned. You could examine Roberta's feelings as she matures and what motivates her behavior.

History and Context

One way to explore "Recitatif" is through an exploration of the historical context of the short story. The racial conflicts that are integral to the story's plot help define the characters and the ways they view themselves and others. You could also situate the story within Morrison's body of work to draw connections to her other fiction.

Sample Topics:

1. **Busing:** How does busing as a tool of desegregation play a role in the story?

   In an essay you might first look up the busing of students into school districts in order to integrate the American school system. The protagonists, Roberta and Twyla, grow up to be socially aware because of their experiences. As they age and their views diverge, Roberta's political action against busing enrages Twyla.

2. **The climate of "Racial Strife":** How does the racial strife that "came . . . that fall" affect the characters?

The protests against busing are mentioned above, and the overall racial tension in the story creates a particular set of conflicts for the narrator, her friend, their mothers, and the girls at the shelter. Race plays a role in the girls' interactions, but we are never completely sure which race each girl is.

Philosophy and Ideas

Addressing the philosophies in the text is an effective way to address certain social movements and the beliefs people held at particular historical moments. Some of the concepts you could address are racial inequality, group violence, the individual's responsibility to speak up, and the effectiveness of protest.

Sample Topics:

1. **Diverging memories:** How does the story address the issue of the two girls' diverging memories?

The fascinating story about Maggie speaks volumes about memory, people's relationship to the past, and the way the past can be used as a weapon. Roberta and Twyla both remember their stay at the shelter in different ways. You could write about the fact that both struggle with the memory of Maggie's race, which illuminates the ambiguity of Twyla's and Roberta's races.

2. **The individual versus the group:** How does Morrison describe the strengths of communal activity and the downside of conforming to a group?

Roberta remembers the girls joining together to harass and hurt Maggie. Twyla remembers a different outcome to that story. In another instance of group cohesion, the women who picket all come together to make their voices heard. Decide what you think Morrison is saying about group decisions, the strength some people garner from the group, and the importance of having a belief as an individual and remaining true to it.

Form and Genre

The genre is the type of work, in this case fiction, and the form is the structure of the work, in this case a short story told with a narrative voice that goes from that of an eight-year-old child to an adult. In an essay you should look for the many literary devices that the author uses to create and inform the narrative (such as allusions to historical moments and the racial ambiguity of the characters). What else shapes the story? How do we get to see into the characters' minds, and what effect does this have on the reader?

Sample Topics:

1. **The short story form:** How does the short story form affect the narrative?

   Most of Morrison's fiction is in the form of the novel. This short story provokes a lot of discussion in spite of its brevity. How do we get to know characters differently in this short story from those in *Tar Baby*, for example, the novel written just before "Recitatif"?

2. **Point of view:** What is the effect of the first-person point of view in the story?

   Twyla is a child narrator who develops into an adult in the span of the story. How does the language change, as she grows older? In an essay you could explore the naïveté of Twyla's mother in contrast to Twyla's wisdom even though she is so young.

Language, Symbols, and Imagery

An author's language choices for particular characters or during certain moments in the story can shed a lot of light on the narrative. Look at the way figurative language is used to say something about a concept. Rather than just listing the many symbols in the story, try to imagine what the symbols reveal about certain situations or people.

Sample Topics:

1. **Figurative language: metaphors/similes/personification/ symbols:** What does the apple orchard come to mean to the characters?

   In an essay about symbolism, you could examine the words used when Twyla talks about the outside space and the occurrences there.

2. **Repetition of words, sounds, and images:** Twyla repeats that she and Roberta do not have "beautiful dead parents in the sky." What is the dramatic effect of this repetition?

   Throughout the story, Roberta and Twyla struggle to find their place in the world. The seeds of their disconnectedness are perhaps planted when they are abandoned as children. You could look at the ways their parents shame them, and how they feel unfortunate even though they have mothers because of their mothers' neglect.

3. **The significance of the title:** How does the title relate to the characters and their experiences?

   Find the definition of the title, and decide the connection that the definition has to various events and characters' lives. What is the significance of the musical reference?

Bibliography for "Recitatif"

Mills, Nicolaus, ed. *The Great School Bus Controversy.* New York: Teacher's College P, 1973.

Wicker, Tom. *Tragic Failure: Racial Integration in America.* New York: William Morrow, 1996.

BELOVED

READING TO WRITE

MEMORY IS integral to the plot of the Pulitzer Prize–winning novel *Beloved*, and the simultaneous acts of both remembering and repressing painful memories are exemplified by Morrison's story-telling techniques. A writer could focus on memory and its myriad aspects and could explore what it is exactly that the characters are trying to repress and why their efforts are unsuccessful. Isolating specific scenes that focus on memory loss or recovery would be the place to start if writing on that topic. Identifying what the novel is saying about memory is the next step. Relating the theme to character development, the techniques Morrison uses, and the effects on the reader, for example, are all ways to take the discussion further. Because Sethe assumes that Beloved is a transient with amnesia resulting from the trauma of slavery or from some other form of abuse, she asks Beloved if she has "disremembered" (118) the details of her past. The question produces dramatic irony, since the reader believes Beloved is Sethe's ghost child returned in the flesh. Beloved could also be a transient person, giving rise to further complexity in the novel. Perhaps more than Beloved, the person who has truly "disremembered" her life is Sethe. An essay could analyze Sethe's memories as the novel unfolds, and the ways readers are left to evaluate Sethe's actions in the context of her "unspeakable" past (58).

Close reading of a passage—when a reader analyzes the meanings of details in a piece of literature—helps the reader isolate the author's carefully chosen images and see what they might mean in the larger context of the novel. The tense dialogue that Paul D and Sethe have about her act of infanticide provides lots of material for an essay. The conversation includes many philosophical ideas such as the difficulties that characters face with communicating their feelings, and the ongoing conflicts that they struggle to overcome:

> Suddenly [Paul D] saw what Stamp Paid wanted him to see: more important than what Sethe had done was what she claimed [that her act would provide her children with safety]. It scared him.
>
> "Your love is too thick," he said thinking, That bitch is looking at me; [Beloved] is right over my head looking down through the floor at me.
>
> "Too thick?" she said, thinking of the Clearing where Baby Suggs' commands knocked the pods off horse chestnuts. "Love is or ain't. Thin love ain't love at all."
>
> "Yeah. It didn't work, did it? Did it work?" he asked.
>
> "It worked," she said.
>
> "How? Your boys gone you don't know where. One girl dead, the other won't leave the yard. How did it work?"
>
> "They ain't at Sweet Home. Schoolteacher ain't got em."
>
> "Maybe there's worse."
>
> "It ain't my job to know what's worse. It's my job to know what is and to keep them away from what I know is terrible. I did that."
>
> "What you did was wrong, Sethe."
>
> "I should have gone on back there? Taken my babies back there?"
>
> "There could have been a way. Some other way."
>
> "What way?"
>
> "You got two feet, Sethe, not four," he said, and right then a forest sprang up between them; trackless and quiet.
>
> Later he would wonder what made him say it. The calves of his youth? or the conviction that he was being observed through the ceiling? How fast he had moved from his shame to hers. From his cold-house secret to her too-thick love (164-65).

This long climactic passage gives the reader a lot to consider for an essay. Because of laws restricting slaves from being educated, neither Paul D nor Sethe can fully read the newspaper article that Paul D shows Sethe, but their philosophical discussion of infanticide is no less intellectual, thought-provoking, and emotional.

The effects of both love and oppression on the human spirit, keeping and avoiding the painful secrets of the past, and harboring regrets and hoping for deliverance are just some of the many ideas that can be identified in the above passage and analyzed further. This is the only time in the novel when Sethe actually talks about killing her child, and even then, she does not ever say the words or describe the scene. Other characters describe the actual act. Why does Morrison tell the story of the infanticide in this manner? Can readers imagine Sethe's motivation? Sethe claims she is saving her children from the horrors of Sweet Home; although Paul D has experienced those very horrors, and has seen Sixo burned alive, for example, he still suggests that going to Sweet Home might not be the worst fate. Why does he say this? The comments about love are equally fascinating, and can be looked at in depth in relation to other conversations about love in the rest of the novel.

In an ironic twist, Paul D tells Sethe that she "got two feet, . . . , not four" thus suggesting that her act was that of an animal. His language reiterates the slave masters' views that the African Americans were beasts, and this is another motif (a recurring image that presents a thematic idea) in the novel. As soon as he says the words, he connects his accusation and condemnation to his own shame, another recurring thematic idea that might lead to an interesting essay. The figurative "forest" that obscures their love for each other after this exchange is just one more motif that persists throughout the novel. Trees—symbolically representing strength, beauty, life, mystery, growth, and of course the physical structures that were used to suspend the bodies of punished slaves—are an integral part of the landscape and of many of the characters' lives.

When Paul D is on the coffle, he feels that "Life was dead. . . . Or so he thought" (109). The novel explores life after death, both figuratively and metaphorically. The non-linear narrative illustrates, among other things, the difficulties people have with coming to terms with such inhumane conditions. Morrison shows us the human body enduring the worst indignities and surviving physically, as Sethe and Paul D do, in contrast to Paul A's demise; he is hanged for attempting to escape. Emotional survival is another matter. Baby Suggs urges her followers to love their bodies and themselves, which the main characters of this novel try to do.

TOPICS AND STRATEGIES

Here you will find a variety of topics to consider. It is up to you to inter-pret the events and characters in the novel in an original way. Doing your own research can help you to situate some of the occurrences in the novel into historical context and can also help you to identify a unique approach to the novel.

Themes

The themes in the novel are many, and can be explored in an essay in combination with subjects discussed in the closely related Philosophy and Ideas section (see below). Once you have distinguished a theme that you would like to investigate further, establish what the novel is saying about that theme. The themes can often be isolated by paying attention to recurring symbols, words, ideas, and images. People's hearts and the color red (obvious symbols of love) are repeatedly focused on throughout the novel, so an essay could explore love. After identifying the theme of love, you could then look at people's attempts to repress feelings of love and longing because of the harsh conditions of slavery that stripped people of their humanity. Parenting, loneliness, and social ostracism are examples of themes that characters experience simultaneously, often presenting themselves in a cause/effect manner. For example Sethe's har-rowing choices as a parent (and the community's reaction to her choices) lead to her surviving daughter's loneliness and isolation. In an essay you can also relate the themes to the plot and the way events are revealed to the reader. What roles do people's regrets and misgivings about the past, for example, play in their lives, and how are these past instances revealed or remembered?

Sample Topics:

1. **Violence:** How are some of the violent acts in the book revealed, and is recovery for the characters involved possible?

Violence was at the core of the system of slavery, and made it possible for the system of racial servitude to flourish and continue for over 200 years. For an essay on the numerous occurrences of violence, you could incorporate research into the violent nature of slavery and how Morrison presents that reality in the lives of these characters. You could also explore the ways the violence is described. Much of the violence is hinted at, or referred to through euphemism, or with a symbol that may tell only a fraction of the story. For example, Stamp Paid finds a piece of scalp with a red bow attached to the hair, and keeps and caresses the ribbon. Why are we not given the whole story behind the symbolic red ribbon and the horrific occurrence it represents?

2. **Love:** What are the various manifestations of and attitudes toward love, and what creates these viewpoints?

In an essay on this central theme, you may want to consider the actions, thoughts, and conversations of different characters and what they reveal about people's ability (or struggle) to love in dire circumstances. Find examples of how people in the novel show love in many different ways and have varying attitudes toward love. What life experiences lead to their views on love? You may explore the irony of violence and love often coexisting in this cruel world during and after slavery. Sethe's violent act could be juxtaposed to Beloved's voracious appetite for love in an essay that examines the cause and effect of Sethe's actions. Baby Suggs's mantra to "[l]ove your flesh" (88) is fascinating if juxtaposed with Paul D's statement that "[t]o love anything that much was dangerous" (45) and Ella's harsh comment to Sethe: "Don't love nothing" (92). The title, *Beloved,* could also be looked at, not as a noun, but as the verb form "to be loved." Do all Morrison's characters need to be loved? In what way?

3. **Escape:** Examine the literal and figurative escapes made in the novel. How else is physical movement a crucial part of many characters' lives?

To address this topic, identify what the characters are actually escaping from, then determine whether the escape is literal, figurative, or a combination of the two. What fuels the desire for freedom, and what does freedom mean to the characters? Your essay could follow the actions of those characters who physically escape and investigate what conditions led them to escape. Paul D calls himself a "walking man" (46), and covers astounding distances on foot, which was not uncommon during and after slavery. What does his restlessness symbolize? What is he walking away from (literally and figuratively), and is he successful? Characters additionally desire freedom from mental torture. Denver's anguish at watching her mother wither away at the mercy of Beloved preempts her physical movement across town to find some help and to rectify the situation, even though she rarely ventured out of her house. What other physical movements occur that help alleviate (or sometimes cause) people's suffering?

Character

Characterization in this novel is particularly fascinating, given the historical context that reduced African Americans to animal status. Morrison illustrates this viewpoint when we get to see inside the minds of the slave catcher who compares Sethe to the animals in his care. What is Morrison saying about the system of slavery by creating such complex and multifaceted lives for the people who were seen as "creatures" and juxtaposing these lives with those who dehumanized them? Is it possible for the characters to retain their humanity in the face of such mistreatment? Papers can examine character development (such as how Morrison illustrates Baby Suggs's sense of compassion), means of characterization (like the way we learn about Sethe's background from her repressed memories), or interpretations of changes in a character as the novel proceeds (Denver's transformation from isolated to part of the community). This novel is particularly intriguing to write about, because Beloved as a character is dead, then later appears in the flesh (one interpretation), and other characters in the book question her very existence. Morrison challenges the readers' notions of reality throughout the novel, which is typical of much of her work. Examine not only the way the characters are presented to the reader, but also how the characters react in their world, to other characters, and what they represent in the story.

Sample Topics:

1. **Denver's character:** What conditions bring about Denver's loneliness and what are her reactions to Beloved?

At the beginning of the novel, before Denver's transformation, Paul D claims that Denver appears to be waiting for something to happen (41). What is Denver literally and figuratively waiting for, what is the cause of her isolation, and how does she react when Beloved appears? Writing about Denver may also involve analyzing her relationship with her mother, Sethe, whom she seems to be inextricably connected to, forcing her to reverse roles at the end of the novel in which she must provide for the household in the way her mother used to. Denver is also described as being "charmed" (41). What does this mean in the context of the novel's supernatural occurrences?

2. **Paul D's character:** Consider the symbolism of the "tin can" in Paul D's chest and how its eruption causes him to face his painful past.

To write about Paul D, you could focus on the tin can that figuratively opens up in his chest, revealing the past that he endured. Why does he, like Sethe, engage in actively keeping the past at bay? What are some of the occurrences that he figuratively keeps hidden in his chest? Examining the symbols in the novel that are connected to this major character (his heart, his tin can, the trees he talks about) would add to the discussion. An essay on Paul D could also include his physical movement and the ways he physically moves because of Beloved's supernatural effect on him. The significance of his name could also be explored, since he is part of a group of men all with the same first name, and he seems to be the only survivor of these Sweet Home men.

3. **Sethe's character:** Does Sethe survive "the Misery" (171), as Stamp Paid calls her act of infanticide?

In this essay about Sethe, you could include an in-depth look at the role of love in her life. Sethe believes that she is committing an act of love by not returning her child to the confines and violence of slavery. How else do we come to know about Sethe's life? What about her is extraordinary in the context of her past? Sethe believes that she has a "tree on [her] back" (15). How does this belief and others that she maintains help her to cope with her life experiences? Sethe as a dynamic character is interesting to write about in an essay because of the drastic changes she endures throughout the novel. You might also want to focus on her language use, her memories of Baby Suggs, the lessons she learns from her, and her relationships with her other children.

History and Context

Beloved, winner of the Pulitzer prize of fiction in 1988, strengthened Morrison's place as a celebrated American writer. That she was writing about one of America's most shameful atrocities is noteworthy, and this social context could be included in an essay that examines the power of the book itself and the way in which it was received and given accolades by the literary world. Putting *Beloved*'s extraordinary and astonishing events into historical context is another way to approach the novel in an essay. The social environment at the time—one in which African Americans were the victims of chattel slavery in which they could be bought and sold as the property of another person—sounds as incredulous 200 years later as does the story of an irate baby ghost haunting a family and then coming back from death in human form. You could consider the ludicrousness of the ghost story as one way that Morrison illuminates the absurdities of society's beliefs at the time. The injustices that Morrison illustrates seem incredulous when read in the current social climate that espouses equality for all Americans. Further research into the impact of migration, slavery, and the acts that legally sanctioned racism and violence would add another dimension to your essay.

Sample Topics:

1. **Chattel Slavery:** Stamp Paid describes Sethe's act of infanticide as a reaction to the Fugitive Bill of 1850 (171). Put Sethe's
actions into historical context with an exploration of that historical reality and others, such as manumission and antislavery,
or historical figures that Morrison refers to, such as Dred Scott
and Sojourner Truth (173).

A research paper on chattel slavery, the legally sanctioned
ownership of another human being, could take you in many
directions. Decide on a focus, and keep it connected to a
particular character or event from the novel. Look up these
historical events, starting with a book such as John Blassingame's *The Slave Community, Plantation Life in the Antebellum South,* and tie in your research to the occurrences in the
characters' lives. Many of the characters refer to ownership
of another person, so you could relate this idea of the desire
to own another person in a loving way, and the contrast to
the system of legalized ownership. What commentary does
the book make about ownership and the forms in which it is
manifested?

2. **Reconstruction:** Explore the conditions for African Americans in the period following slavery known as Reconstruction (1863 to 1877), and relate the conditions to those that
characters such as Denver, Sethe, Paul D or Stamp Paid
encounter.

An essay on Reconstruction could be narrowed down to a
discussion of some of the historical societies that Morrison
mentions such as the Colored Ladies of Delaware, Ohio, and
the Religious Society of Friends (the Quakers) and their con-
tributions to American society in the aftermath of Slavery.
You might also consult a book such as John Hope Franklin's
From Slavery to Freedom: A History of African Americans.
What commentary is *Beloved* making about the enslaved

people's quality of life once they have been physically emancipated?

3. **The role of the community:** What is the role of the community in the novel, and how is the sense of the collective an integral part of the African-American experience in that historical time period?

Addressing this topic would involve research into the African-American community during and after slavery, and narrowing down a specific focus for your paper. Morrison creates a community in the novel that feels a sense of responsibility for fellow African Americans. Baby Suggs is a community leader whom people respect. What causes the community to distance themselves from Sethe and leave her virtually isolated for decades? Her life situation could be contrasted to Stamp Paid's life and the way he is welcomed into every house in the town.

Philosophy and Ideas

This approach is similar to discussing the novel's themes, but in looking at the philosophies and ideas informing the novel, you are investigating what the novel is saying about the ideas in a more general form. Although the characters have been denied a formal education because of the confines of slavery, they engage in deep philosophical ponderings about the nature and meaning of time, identity, the responsibility of the community to the individual, and personal accountability for one's actions. What is Morrison saying by infusing her characters with such complex thought when they are illiterate in the technical sense, and are viewed by society as being less than human? Many of the philosophies and ideas that can be examined in the book are inextricably linked to characters' relationship to the past. In your discussion of the various life views and philosophies that some characters may have, consider the ways the narrative shifts in time and from character to character and how we learn of the past and their views about it, in spite of characters' reluctance to revisit it. At the heart of the novel is Sethe's act of infanticide, which

Stamp tells Paul D about for the sake of "truth and forewarning" (170). Why is the search for or the avoidance of the truth such an integral part of characters' existence? In the context of slavery and the dire conditions that Sethe and others faced at Sweet Home, what is the novel telling us about the act of mercy killing?

Sample Topics:

1. **Infanticide:** Examine the literal and figurative meanings of Sethe's statement "motherlove was a killer" (132) in connection to characters in the novel.

   In Sethe's internal monologue quoted above, she contemplates Paul D's request to have a baby with him, and the irony of her thoughts is immediately apparent. Another irony is Paul D's attempt to tell her his secret of making love to Beloved, while Sethe herself is harboring her secret about her act of infanticide. The act of "mercy" that Stamp Paid describes as "The Misery" (171) could be viewed from different moral, social, and historical perspectives in your essay. Pay attention to the varying commentaries that we get about Sethe's act. What do they tell us about her desperate situation, since she was actually trying to kill all of her children but did not get the chance? How is the scene described, and from whose point of view do we first get a description of the scene? What are the roles of the community, Paul D, and Stamp Paid?

2. **Time:** "Time never worked the way Sixo thought" (21). How does time "work" in the novel, in terms of people's sense of time, and the timing of events as they unfold in the novel?

   An essay on the literal time that passes in the novel and the unfolding of events could be interesting, and could be related to other considerations of the form and structure of the novel. Time as a construct could also be explored in connection to people's experiences with post-traumatic stress disorder (PTSD). Are their attempts to recover from the past futile? Sethe becomes joyfully immersed in a "timeless present" (184) when she believes Beloved is the child she killed and that she has returned from death full of forgiveness. How do characters cope with the idiosyncrasies of time? Paul D and Stamp Paid, for example, struggle with their painful memories of the past, but no matter how much time has passed, they see these images as if they happened recently.

3. **"Rememory"**: How is a character's memory, or "rememory" as Sethe calls it (36), or lack thereof, related to his or her emotional response to it?

Characters' memories usually come in the form of vivid visual images of the remembrance, which may be revealed to the readers in snippets, then the full impact of the memory and the visual is revealed. Morrison's characters are reluctant to revisit such a painful past and spend a tremendous amount of energy repressing certain parts of their histories. Paul D "had shut down a generous portion of his head" (41). People suffering from post-traumatic stress disorder (PTSD) often struggle with their recollections of the traumatic event. You could research the syndrome in depth in *The Post-Traumatic Stress Disorder Sourcebook* by Glenn R. Schiraldi, and explore if the ways the characters remember seem to be symptomatic of PTSD.

Form and Genre

The structure of *Beloved* continues to fascinate, challenge, and delight readers. An essay could explore the way the narrative unfolds and how the reader is informed of events, ideas, and characters. In this case, the novel form is adapted in interesting ways, and you can explore the way the author uses the form to shape and reinforce the ideas in the work. The antagonistic forces in the novel also shape the novel by influencing the realities of characters. Rather than listing the forces that act against protagonists, examine the source of these forces by looking at whether they are internal or external to the character, and whether they are resolved. How has Morrison as an author purposefully used the complex narrative form to shape *Beloved*? The revelations within the narrative provide clues about some of the mysteries in the book.

At the end of the novel, we see a captivating stream of consciousness from Beloved's point of view. Some critics believe that here we receive evidence that she is a survivor of slavery recalling the horrors of the Middle Passage. One interpretation of her character is that she is not the ghost baby of Sethe returned from the grave but a woman who experienced one of the most violent historical occurrences in human memory. Themes also play a role in the form of the novel, since memory, a major theme, is expressed through the fragmented narrative, allowing us to see the mind at work, struggling to recollect events that are crucial to the character.

Sample Topics:

1. **Point of view:** What purpose does the shifting point of view serve in the narrative?

   In an essay about the point of view, you might investigate the shifts from person to person and from limited omniscient to omniscient to first person points of view. The point of view in the novel is closely related to people's memories and struggle against remembering. Many of the shifts in point of view take us to characters' experiences of the same episode, so we get to see different catastrophic events from many perspectives. Often the varying points of view fill in different details of the incidents, including, for example, Baby Suggs's point of view even though she is dead when the action of the novel begins. We also hear the characters' internal monologue about the very act of remembering memories that they didn't even know that they had. The shift in point of view is also closely tied in with visual imagery. In a section that is presented using a limited omniscient point of view from Stamp Paid's perspective, he says he has "seen too much" (169), underscoring the connection of unsettling visual images to painful memories.

2. **Stream of consciousness:** How do the episodes of stream of consciousness challenge the reader and shed light on the themes, such as memory, loss, and desire?

Stream of consciousness is sometimes employed by an author to allow the reader into the roaming mind of a character during a particularly significant time in his or her life. Beloved's recollections of "being dead," or being enslaved, are fascinating to explore. Take time to reread the episodes that seem to be emotionally charged conversations between Beloved, Sethe, and Denver. What is actually happening and who is saying what? Once you have identified the speakers, you may want to determine how their comments illustrate their desires or beliefs, and what Morrison may be saying about blame, responsibility, and the possibilities for reconciliation and forgiveness.

3. **Antagonists and protagonists:** How does Morrison complicate the notion of protagonists and antagonists in the novel?

Addressing this topic would involve looking at the ways the antagonists, or forces acting against the main characters, can be catalysts for self-knowledge. What negative forces create change? Another approach would be to examine the complicated nature of race relations in the novel and to analyze Baby Suggs's claim that, "there was no bad luck in the world but white-people" (104) and how that reality is presented along with the actions of "benevolent" whites. You could research the institution of slavery and how it was supported by religious institutions, which gave it moral sanction in the community and which insured its continuance.

Language, Symbols, and Imagery

An author usually chooses certain language, symbols, and imagery to convey meaning in a suggested way, rather than a literal way. *Beloved* is rich with figurative language—that which is not to be taken literally—as well as vivid images that are intentionally located and repeated in the narrative, and then their significance explained later. An example of an image that is hinted at in the beginning of the novel is the disturbing image of the boys who hold Sethe down and suck her lactating breasts. Over the course of the novel, as Sethe faces her past more boldly, we come to see the horrific scene in its entirety, seeing not only how it affects Sethe but also how it contributes to Halle's insanity. What other horrific images do we catch a glimpse of from a character who deliberately tries to repress memories? Once you have decided on a significant image, relate it to character development or a point that you think the author is trying to make. Symbols, concrete objects that suggest abstract ideas, can be placed in the novel strategically and repeated for dramatic effect. In an essay, rather than simply listing various symbols that you have identified in the novel, you could show how they connect to a theme or a philosophy of life that a character holds dear. One example worth exploring in an essay could be the many references to Paul D's "tin can" (see above in the Character section), which could be symbolic of his closed-off heart. If you were exploring the meaning of that symbol in reference to Paul D, you could identify what purpose the tin can serves in his life and how his life changes once the can opens up.

Sample Topics:

1. **Figurative language: metaphors/similes/personification/symbols:** There are many examples of personification in the novel. What purpose does it serve in the narrative?

   Avoid simply identifying examples of personification and stating the fact that they exist in many places throughout the narrative. You may want to find one or two related examples, such as the personification of Sweet Home and the house at 124 Bluestone Road and the irony contained therein, and examine the contrasting homes and what they mean to characters. The rooster called Mister that Paul D sees smiling is an interesting example of personification because it is only mentioned a few times, but the image is striking, and speaks volumes to Paul D about the lot of African Americans and the ways they were held in captivity and animalized. Make sure that you tie the instances of personification to a particular theme or to an aspect of character development or the way a character is revealed. Use an in-depth discussion of one or two points rather than a brief discussion of many metaphors.

2. **Imagery:** What are some of the more memorable images in the novel, and why does Morrison employ such horrific imagery?

Personification involves vivid images, and some of the images entail personification, like the vivid images of the human-like trees. There may be some overlap, and indeed they are not always separate and distinct categories. Trees are also symbolic, and you may want to uncover the ways different trees have different meanings for the characters. You could include the vivid images of Sethe's "chokecherry tree" (79) and how these visions are a constant reminder of her harrowing experiences at Sweet Home. Again, simply pointing out the disturbing image is not enough in an essay; you would want to relate the visual to an idea or theme or character development. Color imagery is also important and can be connected to characters' emotional states and their experiences.

3. **Naming:** How do the names in the novel shed light on places and/or characters?

A discussion of naming would avoid listing examples of noteworthy or unusual names, but would instead figure out what the names mean in the larger context of the story. The system of slavery assigned slave masters' names to their slaves as a means of identification and asserting ownership over the person. What purpose did it serve for the enslaved to be left ignorant about their family names? Does this withholding of information present itself in any other aspects of their lives? What power is inherent in the act of naming someone? How can this power or lack thereof be related to Sethe's life (whose mistress Garner insisted on calling her Jenny) or any of the other characters' lives, like the many men who are named Paul?

Compare and Contrast Essays

Comparing and contrasting elements in a literary work can help to illuminate what these differences or similarities mean in the larger context of the novel. Analyzing the differences between places, characters, and philosophies can provide the basis for an interesting essay, as long as the essay does not deteriorate into a list of similarities and differences. Try to connect the similarities and differences to what the novel is saying about a particular theme or idea. You could also compare and contrast ideas, characters, or narrative structure from novel to novel if there is some basis for the comparison or contrast. An analysis of mothering in *The Bluest Eye* and *Beloved*, for example, may unearth a fascinating discovery of the unique conditions faced by Pauline Breedlove and Sethe as they try to raise their daughters in dire social situations. *Beloved*'s stark contrasts, for example Denver's metamorphosis from the beginning of the novel to the end, could also be explored.

Sample Topics:

1. **Sweet Home versus 124 Bluestone Road:** How do the two places provide a sense of security to their inhabitants?

   Contrasting places is interesting, since you could address not only the differences in the physical places, but also what they represent historically, socially, and emotionally for the characters. Bluestone Road, which is a fearful place, also ironically represents the literal freedom of the enslaved: Baby Suggs's freedom was earned by her son Halle who worked to buy his mother's freedom from the "benevolent" Mr. Garner. The house is both a place of freedom and a place of emotional and physical imprisonment for Denver and Sethe. When Paul D arrives, he literally cannot stay in the house, since Beloved's supernatural will forces him out. Examining the name of the slave plantation "Sweet Home" leads to further analysis of the connotations of the name, in juxtaposition to what the slaves experienced there.

2. **Denver Suggs versus Beloved:** How do the "sisters" relate to Sethe?

   Writing about the different ways Denver and Beloved respond to Sethe could include an analysis of the love they exhibit for her. Before she materializes in the flesh, Beloved is described by Baby Suggs as being a ghost who is desperate for love, whereas Denver's sole companion for the majority of her life is her mother. It seems that Denver would benefit from distancing herself from her mother, in contrast to Beloved who cannot seem to be satisfied. Looking at how each young woman develops as a character, the ways they are characterized, and their actions and speech could add to the effectiveness of your analysis.

3. **The community versus the individual:** Sethe claims she had "twenty-eight happy days . . . followed by eighteen years of disapproval and a solitary life" (173). Discuss this quotation in the context of Sethe's past and ongoing living conditions.

Putting the importance of the community in African-American life into historical perspective (see the section on History and Context) will help you in an analysis of the contrasting realities. After investigating the effects in Sethe's life of being shunned by the community, what is Morrison saying about belonging? Are Denver's efforts to rejoin the community hopeful? Not only could you contrast Sethe's brief happiness to the challenging life at 124 Bluestone Road, but you could also include a discussion of her life at Sweet Home and the contrasting life she creates for herself once she escapes to freedom.

Bibliography for *Beloved*

Gates, Henry Louis, Jr., and K. A. Appiah, eds. *Amistad Literary Series: Toni Morrison: Critical Perspectives Past and Present.* New York: Amistad Press, 1993.

Blassingame, John. *The Slave Community, Plantation Life in the Antebellum South.* Oxford: Oxford UP, 1972.

Bloom, Harold, ed. *Modern Critical Interpretations. Toni Morrison's* Beloved. Philadelphia: Chelsea House Publications, 1998.

Franklin, John Hope. *From Slavery to Freedom: A History of African Americans.* 8th ed. New York: Knopf, 2000.

Iyasere, Solomon O., and Marla W. Iyasere, eds. *Understanding Toni Morrison's* Beloved *and* Sula: *Selected Essays and Criticisms of the Works by the Nobel Prize–Winning Author.* New York: Whitston Publishing, 2000.

Lee, Rachel. "Missing Peace in Toni Morrison's *Sula* and *Beloved*," *African American Review* 28, no. 4 (1994): 571–83.

Mbalia, Doreatha Drummond. *Toni Morrison's Developing Class Consciousness.* 2d ed. Selinsgrove, PA: Susquehanna UP, 2004.

Schiraldi, Glenn R. *The Post-Traumatic Stress Disorder Sourcebook.* Lincolnwood, IL: Lowell House, 2000.

JAZZ

READING TO WRITE

THE UNCONVENTIONAL structure of *Jazz* might be a place to start when thinking about writing about the novel. The shift in the tense and point of view and the repetition of words and concepts all contribute to making the narrative feel nonlinear. Chapters and episodes often start with a main idea, depart on tangent, then return to the main idea. As a writer, you can identify the main storyline, then note when episodes or characters' memories deviate from it. You could discuss the effectiveness of this method and what the structure might be illustrating about characters or events. There are many references to jazz music, and it is personified throughout the text: It actually exerts control over people's bodies when they dance, for example. Many critics have argued that the novel emulates a piece of jazz music, noting that the word *jazz* is never actually mentioned in the book but that the narrative follows the form of a jazz composition. Other critics dispute this claim and prefer to describe the narrative structure as circular rather than as a piece of jazz music.

Writing about the form of *Jazz* leaves you with much to consider about the novel. You could focus on the repetition of ideas and names from Morrison's other novels or the ways specific characters recollect events. The novel opens almost as if in mid-sentence or in the middle of a thought and continues as if the narrator is engaging in a conversation with the word "Sth." This utterance can be found in the middle of *Beloved*: As Stamp Paid stands outside 124 Bluestone Road, he thinks of "a sth when she misses the needle's eye. . . . Just that eternal, private conversation that takes place between women and their tasks"

(172). There are other references in *Jazz* to Morrison's earlier novels in the text, such as the repetition of many characters' names. The name *Dorcas* from *Song of Solomon* (and also in Alice Walker's *Meridian*), for example, shows up in *Jazz*. Not only are names repeated, but also the situations characters find themselves in. Margaret Street in *Tar Baby* suffers from dementia and is afraid to talk or act for fear of embarrassing herself. Similarly in *Jazz*, Violet Trace has a "renegade tongue," (24) and so she stays silent. Shadrack's return from World War I in 1919 in *Song of Solomon* may be another moment that Morrison echoes in *Jazz* with the references to the war. There is also repetition within the narrative, since chapters begin with a word or two from the last sentence of the previous chapter, adding to the circular structure of the book.

Close reading of a section of the novel helps to identify themes and a focus for your essay. You might want to go to a section of the novel that is a pivotal point in the plot in order to find characters' motivations. In the following passage towards the end of the novel, we finally get a glimpse of the fateful day on which Joe Trace kills Dorcas Manfred:

> Joe is wondering about all this on an icy day in January. He is a long way from Virginia, and even longer from Eden. As he puts on his coat and cap he can practically feel Victory at his side when he sets out armed, to find Dorcas. He isn't thinking of harming her, or, as Hunter had cautioned, killing something tender. She is female. And she is not prey. So he never thinks of that. He is hunting for her, though, and while hunting a gun is as natural a companion as Victory. (180)

By the time we arrive at this passage in the novel we have a clear sense of Joe Trace's search for his mother and the extent of his suffering and deprivation. Do Joe's life circumstances help the reader to understand his motivations? Does the reader get an explanation of the murder from this final glimpse into the fateful day? What is contradictory about Joe's belief that Dorcas "is not prey" in light of his actions? The irony of Joe's intentions versus his actions is apparent and could be the focus of an essay.

Joe's past may be compared to Golden Gray's search for his identity, and Gray's racial confusion could be another interesting way to approach the novel. Other themes inherent in this passage are friendship (Joe's reliance on Victory) and the importance to the narrative of hunting and stalking. The wordplay in this section—the reference to Victory, the person and the concept, is an interesting aspect of *Jazz* that could be explored. Morrison's reputation as a sophisticated wordsmith can be addressed in an essay on the language used in the text.

Jazz is often compared to *Beloved* because Morrison claims that they are part of a trilogy, with *Paradise* completing the trilogy. You may put the novel into the context of when it was published, and look at *Beloved* and *Jazz* together to ascertain any similarities in theme, philosophy, or unfolding of events or you may include *Paradise* in your analysis to uncover the commonalities among these three great works.

TOPICS AND STRATEGIES

Here you will find a variety of topics to consider. It is up to you to interpret the events and characters in the novel in an original way. Doing your own research can help you to situate some of the occurrences in the novel into historical context and can also help you to identify a unique approach to the novel.

Themes

Writers can identify themes in a work of literature by paying attention to repeated or emphasized words, ideas, and patterns of behavior, since all of these may suggest themes or concepts in the novel. Once you have identified a theme, try to uncover what the novel is saying about the theme. In *Jazz*, there is a lot of repetition of the effects of music, the community, and race on the city dwellers. Many of the themes are integral to the African-American migratory experience from the south to the north, and from the country to New York. The city plays a role in most of the themes in the novel, so a consideration of violence, for example, could be put in the context of the personified city, and how the city might contribute to, or create, people's anger and fury. When writing about theme, you may write about connected themes, such as abandonment and fear, and you may find some of your themes blending with the Philosophies and Ideas suggestions that are explored in the later section.

Sample Topics:

1. **Music and the city:** In what ways is music (which appears in many forms in the novel) personified, connected to the personified city, and held responsible for people's actions?

   Writing about the city and music would include identifying when the two are described as being inextricably connected. You could look for situations when a character enjoys or denounces music, and the role music has in influencing a person's thoughts or actions. Music is held responsible for figuratively and literally changing the weather, for influencing people's actions, causing black people to riot, and for causing the "Imminent Demise" (56) of society, among other actions. When Violet and Joe Trace migrate into the city, for example, they arrive dancing on the train, not possibly imagining a future that involves betrayal and murder. How else is music woven into their relationship and its deterioration?

2. **Fear and abandonment:** How does characters' fear of abandonment or loss play a crucial role in their lives?

   Start by identifying characters who are searching for a sense of self, or who feel incomplete because of their abandonment. Analyzing the loss of security, the characters' sense that they are not complete, and maybe relating a character to another one in a similar circumstance, would be the next step in writing your paper. The social context in which the character lives could also shed light on this theme. People are fearful of a number of situations in the text, for example Alice Manfred lives in fear of the city itself. You may want to investigate what the character is ultimately scared of, and if the character overcomes the fear or exacerbates it with his or her actions.

3. **Love:** How do characters express love in the novel?

   To avoid simply listing the different kinds of love (the maternal love Joe Trace wishes for, the ironic love Violet develops

for Dorcas, for example), try to go one step further by analyzing what the implications of the love are in specific social
contexts. Because of the complex nature of the book, the love
relationships are also complex and people's behavior might
appear to be contradictory. Love is also connected to the city,
and the narrator tells us that people in the city have to learn
"[w]hen to love something and when to quit" (9). Why do Morrison's characters seem to be willing to sacrifice so much in
the name of love?

Character

Writing about character could include a discussion of character traits,
how the author shows us a character is a particular way, and the changes
a character undergoes in the course of the novel. Other people in the
book often describe the characters in *Jazz*, and so readers get many perspectives about a character, including perspectives from the omniscient
narrator. Because some of the actions of the characters can be morally
appraised, the reader is often left to evaluate actions and then come to
a conclusion about that behavior. You can investigate what the characters' behaviors mean in that specific social context, and how Morrison
creates believable characters who are often unpredictable. The ways the
stories are told are integral to the characters, also. Point of view plays a
large role in Joe's story—especially when we get to see his story told in
his voice. Music is also integral to character development, so you may
want to explore the ways music is connected to each character that you
write about. Stream of consciousness is a technique that is employed
with many of the characters. You could decipher what they ponder and
how they come to terms with the disappointments in their lives through
that type of internal monologue.

Sample Topics:

1. **Violet Trace's character:** How is Violet developed as a character who is central to the action of the novel?

   Writing about Violet Trace may involve the way we come to
   know about her through her actions, thoughts, the ways others
   describe her, and the names they use (Violent and Violet—thus

depicting her two personalities). Consider the way Morrison creates her character by the way she interacts with others and their reactions to her. It is interesting to note the method Morrison uses of having the narrator tell us important details about a character which are further developed later: "the children of suicides are hard to please and quick to believe no one loves them because they are not really here" (4). What early clues do we get about Violet from that quotation, and in what manner does she change over the course of the novel? Repetition is also an essential part of the way Violet is characterized: The funeral scene is described numerous times throughout the text. You could explore the effect of this repetition and what we learn about her each time the scene is replayed.

2. **Joe Trace's character:** How are Joe Trace's actions at the beginning of the novel accounted for?

Analysis of Joe Trace as a character would involve a discussion of the way his violent act is revealed to the reader throughout the course of the novel. We do not get the events in chronological order and they are not told by the same person, so you could discuss how the murder is revealed. What impact does Joe's past have on him? Does his search for his elusive mother Wild justify or account for his action? Are we as readers left to decide if his actions are justified, or is he judged in the book? Does the reader feel sympathy for him? His eyes are mentioned many times, and the different colors and the significance of this could be examined.

3. **Dorcas Manfred's character:** How does Dorcas become the sole focus of Joe and Violet's life?

Discussing Dorcas as a character could begin with the effects she has on the lives of Joe and Violet. Her passive acceptance of life as it unfolds could be contrasted to both Joe's and Violet's perseverance and drive. Her name is repeated many times; how do the repetition and obsession that Joe and Violet have for her turn her into a mystical figure? The "wood chip" in her stomach (61) could be compared to Paul D's tin can from *Beloved*. What does it represent for Dorcas? How do her physical attributes take center stage in her life?

History and Context

One way to explore the riches of *Jazz* is through an exploration of the historical context of the novel. Written in 1992, this was the novel Morrison published just before winning the Nobel Prize in literature. *Beloved*, which won the Pulitzer prize for fiction, was written five years previously, and *Jazz* was highly awaited. Many of the themes in *Beloved* continue in *Jazz*. Both explore love in its many forms, and the unanticipated murder of a character's loved one: Sethe's murder of her infant child, to protect her from the horrors of slavery, and Joe Trace's murder of Dorcas. Both novels are based on an actual historical event—*Beloved* on Margaret Garner's murder of her baby, and *Jazz* on a story about a young woman shot by her lover who did not reveal his identity while she lay wounded. Both novels also reveal the horrors of the system of slavery and the psychic and social aftereffects of such a brutal system of oppression. In an essay you may also want to consider the way music provides a context for the characters' lives, and how New York, and specifically Harlem, in the 1920s is described. In historical context, New York in the 1920s played a major role in the production of African-American art forms and the newly created art form of jazz. Putting events and characters into historical context could produce many thoughtful essays.

Sample Topics:

1. **African-American migration to New York City:** How do the historic migrations of African Americans from the South to the northern cities, including New York City, play a role in the novel?

   You might research the opportunities for work for African Americans who migrated to big cities during the late 1800s. Often the work was limited to domestic work for women and sales work for men. You could contrast the big city work to the cotton picking and heavy manual labor that Violet remembers doing in spite of her gender. The parade to celebrate the 369th colored regiment's return from World War I in 1919 (129) is another interesting example of the historical moments that Morrison captures in *Jazz*. There are other historical realities that Morrison includes that give the reader a clear sense of the cultural climate: the brutal Jim Crow laws, color prejudice among African Americans, and unfair sharecropping practices could all be researched and put in the context of the novel and in the context of the characters whose lives are most affected by them, such as Golden Gray and Rose Dear.

2. **The Cult of True Womanhood and feminism:** What examples of feminist sensibilities are present in the novel?

You may approach this essay topic in a variety of ways. The first wave of feminism began in the 1840s and continued until the 1920s, after women gained the right to vote in 1920. Another victory of this historic time was women's right to birth control. Alice Manfred's character seems like an interesting character to explore with regard to gender issues in the novel. She succumbs to her own repression which probably stemmed from the Cult of True Womanhood that existed in the 1800s, which claimed that women should be submissive, pure, domestic, and religious beings. Alice takes part in controlling her niece Dorcas's life, making sure she does not have a "life-below-the-sash" (60) in order for her to avoid the ultimate shame for a young woman: becoming pregnant in a time when birth control was not an option. You could also look at the role of Christianity in the way women were expected to act. Historically, women's clubs helped women to imagine that they could exist in society as equals, and provided the support women needed in this political struggle and in everyday matters.

3. **African-American Societies such as the Universal Negro Improvement Association (UNIA) and the National Negro Business League (NNBL):** What role do various societies have in the novel?

The novel illustrates the historical context that saw African-American upward mobility and the beginnings of a black middle class. There are references to the early protests by the National Association for the Advancement of Colored People (NAACP). The Universal Negro Improvement Association (UNIA) and the National Negro Business League (NNBL) were also trying to improve conditions for blacks at the time that the novel is set. Community leaders such as Booker T. Washington and the religious leader Father Divine are also mentioned. How does the story of Golden Gray's upbringing and the internalized hatred he holds add to the discussion of the role race played in people's lives during slavery?

Philosophy and Ideas

By the time *Jazz* had been published, Morrison's work had been interpreted and analyzed by literary critics, historians, and philosophers who provided various interpretations of the philosophical ideas found in her works. *Jazz* addresses some of the major philosophies of the novels that came before it. The individual's desire to belong and to establish an identity, as well as the rejection felt in love are among the issues that could be analyzed. The nameless narrator of the novel continuously engages in a conversation with the reader in which ideas and life philosophies are discussed, even if those ideas conflict with a character's beliefs or actions. The narrator tells us about the strong allure of the city and says of Violet and Joe, "how soon country people forget. . . . When they fall in love with a city" (33). This quotation could be used to discuss the ideas of loyalty, love, and the importance of geographical place. A discussion of the philosophies in the novel may include certain social movements and the beliefs people held at particular historical moments. Some of the concepts you could concentrate on include racial inequality in the text, the denunciation of certain forms of music, perceived insanity, murder, and people's responsibility when witnessing acts of passion.

Sample Topics:

1. **Violence against women:** How does the novel treat the reality of violence against women?

You could explore the obvious examples of violence geared toward women, then explore the responses women and men have to the violence. Alice Manfred and Violet Trace talk about the class differences inherent in their society that distinguished between upper and lower class women. Alice calls the lower class women, "women with knives" (85), and these women are characterized as fighting back against the violence that is aimed at them.

2. **Post-traumatic stress disorder (PTSD):** Which characters in the novel could be said to suffer from post-traumatic stress disorder (PTSD), and what are their realities?

PTSD could be written about in connection to people's rage and fury after a traumatic event and their sense of loss and abandonment (see the Theme section above). Golden Gray feels the abandonment from his father like an amputee (159), as does Neola Miller, whose arm is paralyzed after the loss of her love (60). The tears people shed are also emphasized, and their desire to kill, stemming from the shame of the traumatic event. Both Golden Gray and Joe Trace want to kill their father and mother respectively, once they have figured out who they are. Does Morrison extend any judgment on the characters' behaviors, or on the perpetrators of the trauma?

3. **Decision making:** What role does decision making play in the novel? Who struggles with decisions?

Decisions are difficult for many of the characters. You could examine the challenging time certain characters have with making important decisions in their lives. When writing about these decisions, you could pick out interesting examples and then investigate what the decision tells us about the characters or their development. For example, when Golden Gray eventually decides to return to the Wild woman and help her, how is that action connected to societal expectations, his upbringing, and his quest to kill his father?

Form and Genre

Much has been written about the form of the novel *Jazz,* with some critics maintaining that the novel is structured like a piece of jazz music, and
others suggesting that the novel follows techniques employed by many
other modernist and postmodernist writers, such as Virginia Wolfe,
William Faulkner, and Gabriel García Márquez. The techniques Morrison uses include a fragmented narrative, where she provides part of the
details of the funeral, for example, then slowly combines the pieces of
Dorcas's murder until the reader has a clear sense of the event and characters' motivations. The form or structure of the novel is also informed
by the narrative voice. Much speculation has been made about the identity of the narrator, and your own ideas on this could make up part of
your essay. Some critics believe the narrator is a character in the novel;
others believe it is the city, music, or the book talking to readers, among
other ideas. In an essay, you should look for the many literary devices
that the author uses to create and inform the narrative (such as allusions
to different songs and music). What else shapes the novel? How do we get
to see into many characters' minds (including that of a murderer and the
person who is murdered), and what effect does this have on the reader?

Sample Topics:

1. **Narrative voice:** How do Violet's narrative voice and stream of
   consciousness shape the novel?

   Violet Trace's thoughts allow us to see into the mind of someone who is labeled as being insane by the community. Try to
   identify what motivates her, and how her human frailty comes
   out through her actions. She certainly experiences internal
   conflict, and is one of many characters who is motivated by
   fury and frustration. Her confusion becomes apparent, and
   the episode that involves her stream of consciousness (95)
   could be examined in the context of her character and what
   she has experienced up to that point.

2. **Point of view:** What is the purpose of the shifts in point of view
   in the novel?

The various points of view could be studied and written about in an essay on the shifting perspectives in the novel. By creating many different stories of people who are all in some way related to Violet and Joe, Morrison allows the reader to take part in this narrative that is woven like a tapestry, with all the characters being connected in some way. The shifting point of view allows us to see different interpretations of the same event and also allows us to go back in time and into the future from the main conflict.

3. *Jazz* **as a piece of jazz music:** How does the novel seem to imitate the form of a piece of jazz music?

Many fascinating articles and books follow the way the novel is almost a recreation of jazz music. Some critics also believe that the narrative structure, replete with repetition, raising an idea then returning to it, is simply novelistic and not connected to any specific musical form. For an essay on this topic, investigate the various arguments that privilege jazz, and those that state that the musical form is not used to create her narrative.

Language, Symbols, and Imagery

An author's language choices for particular characters or moments in the book can shed a lot of light on those actions or moments. Look at the way figurative language is used to say something about a concept. Rather than just listing the many symbols in the book, try to imagine what the symbols say about certain situations or people. A lot of the language in the text is connected to music, such as song lyrics and song titles. Some of the song titles like "I'm So Lonesome I Could Die," the famous song by Hank Williams mentioned on page 119, tell us volumes about the struggles that characters face.

Sample Topics:

1. **Figurative language: metaphors/similes/personification/symbols:** What examples of symbolism are present in the novel and what do they suggest?

Symbols, concrete objects that represent abstract ideas, are prevalent in *Jazz*. Try to uncover what the symbols are and what they represent. The city, symbolic of people's hopes for the future, as well as their failed dreams, is also personified as a decisive character, and this could be contrasted to characters' indecisiveness. You may want to address the symbolism of the knife-wielding people in the text, the birds that Violet releases, and the tears that people cry.

2. **Repetition of words, sounds, and images:** Dorcas's name is repeated many times throughout the text, as are other words. What is the purpose of the repetition?

After identifying repetition, show the emotional state of the character who gets fixated on the word or image. Dorcas, for example, becomes the object of affection for both Joe and Violet. The story begins with her death, but she is not at all dead in the minds of Joe, who cries openly for months, and Violet, who seems to become another person after she tries to attack Dorcas' body at the funeral. Explore why the actual funeral is repeated many times, all from different perspectives, and with different details.

3. **Conversation:** Explore the various conversations that Alice Manfred and Violet Trace have. How do the two women interact with each other?

Alice and Violet's conversations are philosophical in nature and allow the two women a closeness that neither anticipated. Violet goes to Alice's to find a place "to sit down," she claims (80), and ends up with a figurative place to rest her emotions. You could also consider the actions of the two when in each other's company. Alice, who is still trapped in the role of the woman as domestic provider, carefully stitches Violet's clothes that have holes in them or are ripped. What do Alice's meticulous invisible stitches represent?

Bibliography for *Jazz*

Gates, Henry Louis, Jr., and K. A. Appiah, eds. *Toni Morrison: Critical Perspectives Past and Present.* Amistad Literary Series. New York: Amistad P, 1993.

Bloom, Harold, ed. *Toni Morrison's* Jazz. Bloom's Modern Critical Interpretations. Philadelphia: Chelsea House, 1999.

Hardack, Richard. "'A MUSIC SEEKING ITS WORDS': Double-Timing and Double-Consciousness in Toni Morrison's *Jazz.*" *Callaloo* 18, no. 2 (1995): 451–71.

Middleton, David L., ed. *Toni Morrison's Fiction: Contemporary Criticism.* New York: Garland, 1997.

Nowlin, Michael. "Toni Morrison's *Jazz* and the Racial Dreams of the American Writer." *American Literature* 71, no. 1 (1999): 151–74.

Peach, Linden, ed. *Toni Morrison: Contemporary Critical Essays.* New York: St. Martin's, 1998.

Pici, Nicholas F. "Trading Meanings: The Breath of Music in Toni Morrison's *Jazz.*" *Connotations* 7, no. 3 (1997–98): 372–98.

THE NOBEL LECTURE

READING TO WRITE

I N 1993, the Nobel Committee bestowed on Toni Morrison the Nobel Prize in literature, recognizing her work with the most prestigious literary prize in the world. In her Nobel lecture, given December 8, 1993, at Stockholm Concert Hall in Stockholm, Sweden, Toni Morrison said that "word-work is sublime." This lecture allows us into the world of a wordsmith of such caliber, and offers us further appreciation of the high intellectual quality of her work. The lecture comes in the form of a story, reinforcing the worth she gives to "the work [she does] that has brought [her] to this company" as the recipient of the Nobel Prize in literature from the Swedish Academy. The lecture explores the uses and misuses of language and power and the interconnectedness of all people, particularly those of different generations. These basic ideas could be explored in an essay and could be connected to her novels, which also analyze these topics in various ways.

In the speech, Morrison tells a story that is part of the folklore of different cultures. The story highlights issues that can be found in her works of fiction: the ways people of different cultures are marginalized, oppressed, and made the targets of hostility, the ways older people are treated in the same way, and the ways younger people are mistrusted. She relates the old woman in the myth to a writer, and the bird in the myth to language. When writing about the speech, you could connect the use of her metaphors to the many examples of figurative language that Morrison employs in her work, often to make a point, often to illuminate the beauty of language itself.

Putting the speech in the context of the six novels she had written at the time will enable you to write about the speech while keeping in mind the kinds of language, narrative, and content choices she had already made with those novels. Her discussion of language includes the comment: "The vitality of language lies in its ability to limn the actual, imagined and possible lives of its speakers, readers, writers. Although its poise is sometimes in displacing experience it is not a substitute for it. It arcs toward the place where meaning may lie." People often look to literature to help us understand human experiences. Morrison's work surely deepens our awareness and understanding of the emotional and physical lives of humans, but she would say that the novels are obviously not meant to replace those experiences, but to come as close to them as possible. Morrison's writing also departs from people's everyday experiences by including fantasy elements, myth, and folklore. Morrison would probably also claim that the readers of her work have the responsibility of finding "the place where meaning may lie" and not simply expecting the literature to do it for them.

Morrison goes on to expound on the responsibility of language:

Language can never "pin down" slavery, genocide, war. Nor should it yearn for the arrogance to be able to do so. Its force, its felicity is in its reach toward the ineffable.

Be it grand or slender, burrowing, blasting, or refusing to sanctify; whether it laughs out loud or is a cry without an alphabet, the choice word, the chosen silence, unmolested language surges toward knowledge, not its destruction. But who does not know of literature banned because it is interrogative; discredited because it is critical; erased because alternate? And how many are outraged by the thought of a self-ravaged tongue?

Analyzing a larger section of the speech can help you to make connections to her novels and can enable you to isolate important themes that she felt she needed to share with the academy in Stockholm, Sweden, and the world. At the beginning of this large passage she anthropomorphizes language by giving it the human characteristic of arrogance. What you could do is find an example of language (or silence) that Morrison uses in one of her novels that "surges towards knowledge" rather than trying to encapsulate the entire experience, such as slavery. One implication of this view is that we can read a work of literature as an attempt to summarize human experiences, including those that are viewed as mystical or magical. Approaching any of Morrison's texts with this in mind could produce interesting interpretations of the text. Morrison also mentions banned literature. Why does Morrison raise this issue? Another way to look at Morrison's work in connection to her comments in this speech would be in light of the literary criticism of it. Some of the criticism has discredited it, and Morrison has said that some of it has discouraged her from writing. The fact that she won the Nobel Prize in literature showed that she did not give up, in spite of some negative criticism, and kept on producing the work in the ways she imagined, not allowing herself to form a "self-ravaged tongue" that silenced her talent.

TOPICS AND STRATEGIES

Here you will find a variety of topics to consider. It is up to you to provide your interpretation of the speech, and to apply it to Morrison's fiction if appropriate. Doing your own research can help you to situate the speech into historical context and can also help you to identify a unique approach to the speech.

Themes

Writers can identify themes in a work of literature by paying attention to repeated or emphasized words and ideas, since all of these may suggest themes or concepts in the writing. Once you have identified a theme, try to uncover what the speech is saying about the theme. When writing about theme, you may write about connected themes, such as aging and respect, and you may find some of your themes blending with the Philosophies and Ideas suggestions that are explored in the later section.

Sample Topics:
1. **Treatment of the elderly:** What comment does the speech make about the treatment of the elderly in our society?

   Writing about the myth that Morrison alludes to and expounds on would lead you to the stereotypical image of the elderly that the myth exposes. The youth supposedly try to discredit and shame the wise woman by presenting her with a trick question or challenge that she has to solve. Writing about the speech may also include a discussion of the way Morrison looks at the myth in another way. Instead of analyzing it in the typical manner—that the young people are disrespectful and bigoted—she turns the myth around and analyzes the old woman's biased opinion of the young people, and how the woman does not transcend her stereotypical views of them.

2. **Myth:** How does Morrison utilize myth in her speech?

Morrison uses various myths in many of her works, and the myth she refers to is a pleasant inclusion in this formal speech. For an essay you could investigate the myth as archetypal—one that is told in various forms from culture to culture—and the ways the archetypes inform culture. For example the old, wise woman is one archetype, as is the challenge that she receives from the youth—to solve the riddle or puzzle. Traditionally, the ability of the person to solve the high-stakes puzzle is called into question, and immediately the reader aligns himself with the person (in this case the old woman) who is obviously at a disadvantage. Of course, Morrison reverses the archetypal storyline of the youths' desire to discredit the old woman. She reformulates the archetypal story and makes the youth have noble intentions. A writer could look at the end of the rewritten myth, in which Morrison presents the possibilities of reconciliation between the young and the old.

History and Context

Putting Morrison's speech into the context of her accomplishments might be a place to start when looking at her Nobel lecture. The Swedish Academy awarded Morrison the prize because of her stellar body of work. An analysis of the history of the Nobel Prize and of the other Nobel laureates could help you to identify the choices that the Swedish Academy has made historically and whom it has viewed as worthy recipients. Another way to put the speech into context is to analyze the way it addresses similar historical realities as in Morrison's fiction.

Sample Topics:

1. **Morrison's reputation:** What has led to Morrison's being awarded with the most prestigious prize in literature?

Morrison refers to "the work [she does] that has brought [her] to this company." In an essay you could focus on the six novels that Morrison completed before being awarded the prize. You could keep in mind the accolades and awards that her work received, her prestigious teaching positions, and her work as editor that all culminated in the prize. Of course there are literary critics who have not written about all of her work in a favorable way; Morrison says she reads all of the commentary about her work and continues to write regardless of the positive or negative criticism.

2. **Other Nobel lectures:** Put Morrison's speech in the context of other Nobel lectures.

Pick one or two lectures that you feel could be compared to Morrison's lecture. A writer might analyze authors whose styles are similar such as Gabriel Garía Márquez or one who addresses similar themes such as Derek Walcott. In Nadine Gordimer's speech in 1991 she stated:

> In repressive regimes anywhere—whether in what was the Soviet bloc, Latin America, Africa, China—most imprisoned writers have been shut away for their activities as citizens striving for liberation against the oppression of the general society to which they belong. Others have been condemned by repressive regimes for serving society by writing as well as they can; for this aesthetic venture of ours becomes subversive when the shameful secrets of our times are explored deeply.

Morrison's lecture comments on the way writers are silenced by authoritarian governments. Gordimer's speech also has many similarities to Morrison's "The Dancing Mind" speech, which also addresses the fact that writers' lives are often at risk in countries where their work is seen as politically threatening.

Philosophy and Ideas

Morrison's novels are filled with philosophical musings about the nature of human kind—its limitations and its triumphs. The speech's philosophical issues can also be analyzed. When reading a novel, it can be unclear whether or not the author is speaking through the characters, and so the author's intentions are not always apparent. In this speech, Morrison uses characters as a vehicle to convey certain social ideas, but we also get a sense of what philosophical ideas that she as an author finds significant to comment on. When you write about the speech, consider the immediate audience and the fact that Morrison is cognizant that the speech would be disseminated to a worldwide audience and open to multiple interpretations and critiques.

Sample Topics:

1. **Language:** What does the speech say about the role of language in society?

   Writing about language in the speech gives you a lot to consider. Morrison acknowledges that "language . . . tells us . . . how to see without pictures." You could explore how her texts allow the reader to envisage lives through her vivid description. She defines language and claims that it is "a living thing" which can be manipulated and changed, and it is also "an act with consequences." You could look at the various ways language affects people's lives. Morrison laments the fact that language can be used to justify violence, and that it has been used as a form of violence against people.

2. **Obedience:** What does the lecture say about obedience?

Morrison talks about the oppression or silencing of people's language as a tool used "in order to force obedience." The speech condemns societies and governments that oppress and silence citizens' expression. Again, this theme is rampant in her literature. In a way, Morrison has not been obedient to language. She has stretched our comprehension of the world through her use of vernacular and the idiosyncrasies of language which illuminate the complexities of communication.

Form and Genre

Look at the ways Morrison's delivery is different because this is a speech and not a novel. Lectures are traditionally thought of as instructive, allowing the audience a glimpse into the knowledgeable person's mind. People often wonder how authors create whole worlds in their fiction, and what motivates or inspires them to write. Morrison offers some insight into some of her work's recurrent themes and concerns. A lecture also differs from a piece of fiction since there is an audience present who have to be able to hear the words of the speech and understand them orally. Thus the language of a lecture may differ from a written piece, although after the speech is delivered it is often disseminated in the written form. Additionally, an interested person may listen to the actual speech on the Nobel Prize Web site.

Sample Topics:

1. **The lecture format as didactic:** What can an audience learn from the lecture?

   Writing about the pedagogical properties of the speech would involve looking at some of the topics approached above and focusing on those that are informative to the general public. Morrison takes "conventional wisdom" and reimagines it—in the story of the Tower of Babel and in the myth about the old, blind woman. Morrison also does this in many of her novels by reenvisioning myths and conventions.

2. **The lecture as allegory:** How does the allegory challenge the audience?

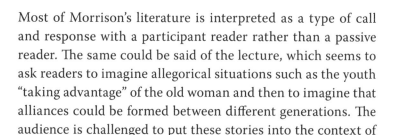

Most of Morrison's literature is interpreted as a type of call and response with a participant reader rather than a passive reader. The same could be said of the lecture, which seems to ask readers to imagine allegorical situations such as the youth "taking advantage" of the old woman and then to imagine that alliances could be formed between different generations. The audience is challenged to put these stories into the context of their own lives—maybe to consider the ways they are prejudiced against older or younger people, for example.

Language, Symbols, and Imagery

Obviously a speech is first and foremost listened to by an audience, then later it may be printed and disseminated in print form. The language used has to be straightforward enough for a listening audience to follow. Writing about the language used could lead you to an exploration of the issues Morrison focuses on and the myths, stories, and allusions that she uses.

Sample Topics:

1. **Allusion:** What is significant about the historical and literary allusions that Morrison makes?

   Morrison's references to Lincoln's Gettysburg Address in 1863 and the biblical story of the Tower of Babel are just two of the allusions that she makes in the speech. These well-known references allow the audience to think about the power of language and the ways languages can divide people.

2. **"Tongue-suicide" and other metaphors:** What is the effect of the metaphors employed in the speech?

   The metaphors in the speech help the listening audience grapple with large issues such as prejudice and the use of language to dominate or subvert societal norms. The comparisons of the bird to language and the woman to a writer help the audience experience the myth in a new way. The silence that Morrison speaks of is central to many of her novels and can be a way for authors to prohibit themselves from

tackling politically sensitive topics in order to avoid repercussions from the government.

Bibliography and Online Resources for the Nobel Lecture

The Nobel Prize Internet Archive: Toni Morrison 1993. Retrieved 23 Jan. 2007
    <http://nobelprizes.com/nobel/literature/1993a.html>
Morrison, Toni. Nobel Lecture 1993. Retrieved 23 Jan. 2007 <http://www.nobel.
    se/literature/laureates/1993/morrison-lecture.html>
Time.com: Read up on Toni Morrison. Updated 21 Jan. 1998. Retrieved 23 Jan.
    2007   <http://www.time.com/time/community/transcripts/chattr012198.
    html>

"THE DANCING MIND" SPEECH

READING TO WRITE

MORRISON GAVE "The Dancing Mind" speech on the occasion of her acceptance of the National Book Foundation Medal for Distinguished Contribution to American Letters, on November 6, 1996. In this speech, Morrison reminds us that "the life of the book world is quite serious. Its real life is about creating and producing and distributing knowledge" (16). Morrison feels that the work engenders responsibility. An essay about her speech could include a discussion of the ways Morrison has taken on the challenges of literature.

Picking a long section of the speech for analysis can help you to focus your argument in an essay. You could, for example, focus on the censure of literature that Morrison alludes to in the following passage, and how this idea of silencing people is echoed in her literary works.

> I know now, more than I ever did (and I always on some level knew it), that I need that intimate, sustained surrender to the company of my own mind while it touches another's—which is reading: what the graduate student taught himself. That I need to offer the fruits of my own imaginative intelligence to another without fear of anything more deadly than disdain—which is writing: what the woman writer fought a whole government to do (15).

Morrison shows us that as a writer she is relatively unscathed: She is not censored; the worst she says she faces is people's derision, whereas the woman writer has to answer to her government, and the opposition she encounters could be a physical threat. You could take this idea and relate it to the comments that literary critics have made about Morrison's literature and the unfortunate repercussions authors have faced for their words.

In that passage and throughout the speech, Morrison connects the act of reading to that of writing. She also claims that reading allows us to delve into our own minds while reading and that the act of reading enables our minds to connect with the author's. An essay might address the ways her novels connect with the readers' lives and maybe also to other authors and novels. Why is it important to be able to sit with the "company of [one's] own mind?"

TOPICS AND STRATEGIES

Here you will find a variety of topics to consider. It is up to you to provide your interpretation of the speech in an essay. Doing your own research can help you to situate the speech into historical context and can also help you to identify a unique approach to the speech.

Themes

Morrison's themes are many and are intricately related in this speech. Some themes may lead you to research the situations writers face in other countries, like the writer whom she met in Strasbourg, France. Once you have identified a theme, try to uncover what the speech is saying about the theme. When writing about theme, you may find some of your themes blending with the Philosophies and Ideas suggestions that are explored in the later section.

Sample Topics:

1. **Reading and writing:** What is the connection between reading and writing, according to the speech?

    "The Dancing Mind" explores the powerful connection between reading and writing and the roles of the reader and the writer. The young student she mentions had not been taught to analyze and internalize what he read, on his own.

He finds great difficulty simply being alone with his thoughts and a text and later on has to learn these skills. Often Morrison's work is described as a challenge for the reader. What would Morrison say about this in light of this acceptance speech?

2. **Power and powerlessness:** How are power and powerlessness associated with language, reading, and writing?

Unfortunately, the writer who pleads with Morrison for help faced physical violence and retaliation for daring to question her society's norms. You could further research the way people's lives can be in danger for writing "against the grain" (12) and how power differentials impel people to question authority. The written word is not viewed as a benign act historically and in many countries, and people are often forced to succumb to the powerful in society (often governments) if they do not appreciate the message in the writing.

Philosophy and Ideas

This speech raises philosophical issues that can also be found in Morrison's novels. The decision to fight against authoritarianism and censorship can be examined in an essay, as well as the society that oppresses in another way—by pressuring its citizens to constantly strive for unrealistic perfection. Other ideas in the speech that could be addressed in an essay are the ways artists create their work and the responsibility we have to ourselves to use our minds.

Sample Topics:

1. **Striving for perfection:** How does striving for perfection in our society often hinder people?

The young man has to learn how to "move outside the surfeit and bounty and excess" (13). Often we view the accumulation of material objects as a positive step, but we do not see the damaging effects it can have on an individual. A paper on the way we strive for more could also include a discussion of the peace reading can create and the importance of challenging the mind.

2. **Social activism and protest:** How does the speech illuminate the significance of social activism and political protest?

In her 1998 *Salon* interview, Morrison says, "You sort of struggle to do four good things when you're my age, and then not deal. I even tell my students that: four things. Make a difference about something other than yourselves." Morrison asks her students to be activists in their daily lives—to help others in some way. The speech also alludes to the significance of cross-cultural alliances and people's responsibility to act—to help others who are facing repression and censorship.

Bibliography and Online Resources for the "Dancing Mind"

Morrison, Toni. "The Salon Interview: Toni Morrison." By Zia Jaffrey. February 1998. Salon.com. Retrieved 20 Jan. 2007 <http://www.salon.com/books/int/1998/02/cov_si_02int.html>

Taylor-Guthrie, Danille, ed. *Conversations with Toni Morrison.* Jackson: UP of Mississippi, 1994.

Time.com: Read up on Toni Morrison. Updated 21 Jan. 1998. Retrieved 23 Jan. 2007 <http://www.time.com/time/community/transcripts/chattr012198.html>

PARADISE

READING TO WRITE

*P*ARADISE, PUBLISHED five years after *Jazz*, completes the trilogy begun by *Beloved*. The multifaceted text poses a challenge to the astute reader who wants to write about this novel. Like many postmodern novels, the text is fractured and the reader has to assemble the numerous strands to form a coherent understanding of the stories. A writer can begin to address *Paradise* by identifying the connections between *Paradise, Beloved,* and *Jazz*.

Beloved, Jazz, and *Paradise* all grapple with a murder that has lasting ramifications for the characters in the novel. In addition, the three novels examine the role of slavery in the lives of African Americans. In *Paradise*, the legacy of slavery has many ramifications and could be explored in an essay. Ruby Morgan's death (113) illustrates the effects of racism and has a lasting impact on the Morgan family and on the community and probably leads to further suspicion of white people and other outsiders. When people do not live up to those expectations, they can be ostracized from the community.

The community's desires also usually surpass the individual's needs. The community makes immense decisions about people's fates, for example, whether or not to call the police when they discover the white family in the car who perished in the blizzard. They end up keeping the law out of their decisions; being self-governing and autonomous was obviously of utmost importance to the founders of Haven and Ruby, and that necessity is inherited. The community is important to the citizens, and this feeling grew out of the betrayal of the "Disallowing" (194) in which

173

their fellow African Americans in Fairly, Oklahoma, would not allow the original people to settle in their all-black town but instead told them to keep on moving to find their own town to live in. Ironically, after being treated this way because of their dark skin color, Ruby's town folks treat outsiders as a threat and are suspicious of any change in the status quo.

The threat from the outside is not the only one the citizens of Ruby face. They also have to cope with the changes that their own inhabitants express:

> Yet there was something more and else in his [Royal's] speech. Not so much what could be agreed with, but a kind of winged accusation. Against whites, yes, but also against them—the townspeople listening, their own parents, grandparents, the Ruby grownfolk. As though there was a new and more manly way to deal with whites. Not the Blackhorse or Morgan way, but some African-type thing full of new words, new color combinations and new haircuts. Suggesting that outsmarting whites was craven. That they had to be told, rejected, confronted. Because the old way was slow, limited to just a few, and weak. This last accusation swole Deek's neck, and, on a weekday, had him blowing out the brains of quail to keep his own from exploding (104).

Examining a long passage like this one can help you to figure out major themes in the book to write about. In the above passage the issue of people's reluctance to embrace change in Ruby is an obvious focus. You could put the passage in the context of the novel, look at whose point of view is privileged in the passage, and in whose section the passage appears. Deacon "Deek" Morgan, the purveyor of tradition, reacts angrily to any suggestion that his ancestors and the current inhabitants of Ruby are approaching life in a less than perfect way. He is unable to take constructive criticism and seems to represent those who are the most resistant to change.

Another theme in the passage is Deek's preoccupation with hunting and the way he uses hunting to release his frustrations. The novel opens with the women in the Convent being hunted, and many times we see Deek's hunting as part of his everyday life. The men decide to disrupt the evil that they believe will permeate into Ruby's social fabric and they settle on storming the Convent and physically rooting out their enemies.

The Convent is a safe place, "free of hunters" Pallas Truelove feels (177); it appears to be the only place where women can go to avoid the harsh dictates of society. It seems to become a paradise for the women just before the men raid the Convent. Ironically, the men of Ruby are described as "good brave men on their way to Paradise" (202).

Literal and figurative sacrifices are other key issues in the book. A victim of severe domestic violence, Mavis Albright literally sacrifices her twins, Merle and Pearl, when she leaves them in the car and they suffocate, because she is on a mission to find the man who abuses her some food to eat for supper. Figurative sacrifice appears in the form of people giving up their beliefs for others. People's sacrifices, the inevitability of change, the way religion is used to influence people could all be examined in essays, along with the form of the novel and the complexity of the narrative structure.

TOPICS AND STRATEGIES

Here you will find a variety of topics to consider. It is up to you to interpret the events and characters in the novel in an original way. Doing your own research can help you to situate some of the occurrences in the novel into historical context and can also help you to identify a unique approach to the novel.

Themes

Writers can identify themes in a work of literature by paying attention to repeated or emphasized words, ideas, or characters' patterns of behavior, since all of these may suggest themes or concepts in the novel. The opening of the novel tells us the number of men carrying out the raid (but they remain nameless until the end of the novel when the mystery is solved) and the number of miles between the town they are in and others. Throughout the novel we see that numbers are important in many ways, and the repetition of the distance between Ruby and other towns tells us the physical isolation of this town as we learn of the social and psychological distance the people feel from others. The men who "shoot the white girl first" and who are "obliged . . . to kill" (3) seem to be hunting the women, which is also a theme that is carried throughout the text. Once you have identified a theme, try to uncover what the novel is saying about the theme. As we learn more about the history of these men, irony abounds when we find out that their ancestors had to flee from maltreatment, but these men are now attacking those whom they view as undesirable. When writing about theme, you may write about connected themes, such as shame and pride, and you may find some of your themes blending with the Philosophies and Ideas suggestions that are explored in the later section.

Sample Topics:

1. **Love:** How do various characters express love?

Writing about the broad topic of love could lead you in many different directions, since love can be tied into almost all of the themes in the novel, and most of the characters' experiences. You could focus on a character who experiences love in different ways, for example Connie's affair with Deacon, which is described as "love in its desperate state" (195), and her deep love for Mary Magna. Who else feels desperation when it comes to the love that they feel? The love need not, obviously, be romantic love, since love also presents itself in the nostalgic feelings characters have for their town and their fond memories of the past that they have difficulty relinquishing. An exploration of the love people have for Ruby and its past could be connected to memory and tradition, for example the love that Arnette and K.D. share presents the possibility of reconciliation for the town of Ruby after the family feud. The love people have for God is another dimension that could be explored in a paper, since divine love is connected to Ruby's history.

2. **Violence:** How does violence transform people's lives in the novel?

Violence shows up in numerous ways, for many reasons, and the perpetrators come in different guises. Some of the violence is historical, so you could explore that in conjunction with ideas such as authority, dominance, and racial superiority. The way the violence is described is also worth looking into, for example on occasion in the novel people are victimized and later on become perpetrators. Violence may not always appear in traditional ways. Is Patricia Best's act of burning the research on the towns' families one of violence? Could the "defective and broken children" that Jefferson and Sweetie Fleetwood lose (191) also be seen as a result of another kind of violence that people face?

3. **Traveling/Walking/Journeying:** How do characters escape from their various experiences in the novel?

Travel is central to many characters' lives, and they often find escape from their past through emotional or physical escape. A lot of the stories that Deacon and Steward Morgan remember are about "[t]he scattering of people" (193). You could explore the recurring motif of journeying by considering the history of Haven and Ruby's founders, what they encountered on their historic journey, and the outcome of their vision for the future. Travel is also an integral part of the lives of some of the characters who end up at the Convent. Such papers on the travelers may include a discussion on the violence the characters are escaping, the walking that is integral to their escape, and their transformation.

Character

Writing about character could include a discussion of the character's traits, how the author has created a particular character, and the changes a character undergoes in the course of the novel. Writing about character involves figuring out how readers get a sense of the characters. You could focus on the ways that unique personality traits allow us to know Morrison's characters. We may feel like we can predict their behavior or not at all. In *Paradise*, a lot of the characters' behavior, interactions, and development are unpredictable and complex. How are the characters in *Paradise* developed? Examining the way Toni Morrison creates her characters and reveals them to the reader can add to your essay. The way each section about a character is told lets the reader know a great deal about that person. Many of the characters are described through the religious lens of Christianity, and these descriptions can tell us a lot about their beliefs, moral values, and whether or not their behavior creates conflict for them.

Sample Topics:

1. **Deacon and Steward Morgan's character:** How do the twins continue the legacy of the patriarchs of their family, their father Rector Morgan and their grandfather Zechariah Morgan?

The twins, who engage in "eternal if silent conversation" (155), seem to act like one person, so they could be examined in an essay as a unit. If you approach the two of them as one character, you could look at their role in the creation of Ruby, the brothers' memories of their father's and grandfather's stories of Ruby's past, and what they are doing to realize their ancestors' mission. You might also consider the importance of hunting to Deacon and the brothers' single-mindedness at the beginning of the novel when they lead the raid on the Convent women. Examining the ways they diverge could add to this discussion. How does Deacon's affair with Connie define him and make his identity divergent from his brother's? At the end of the novel, Connie's murderer is ambiguous. Why does Morrison not tell the reader who pulled the trigger? How is Deacon still responsible even if he is not the one who kills her?

2. **The Convent women's characters: Pallas Truelove, Grace "Gigi" Gibson, Seneca, Mavis Albright, Consolata Sosa:** Pick three of the Convent women and discuss their character development, which leads to their final "enchantment" (283) at the Convent just before it is raided.

Deciphering the motivation for each woman's choice of the Convent as a safe haven would probably be the place to start. Then you could examine their lives in the Convent and how the other women help to transform their lives. Connie seems to feel hatred for the women but ends up transforming all of their lives the most. When Connie has the affair with Deacon Morgan, Penny and Clarisa view Connie's actions "as serious instruction about the limits and possibilities of love and imprisonment" (238). How is this statement a fair one for all of the women's lives, particularly given Connie's rape at age nine? Mavis escapes from domestic abuse and the tragic death of her twins, Merle and Pearl. Seneca is a rape victim—people know she is vulnerable. You could also consider the characters of the townswomen who come in contact with the Convent women, such as Lone, Sweetie Fleetwood, and Soane Morgan. Lone, who teaches Connie how to enter people's bodies and bring them back to life when they are dead, ends up on a mission to save the women from the men's destructive plans and thinks to herself, "Playing blind was to avoid the language God spoke in" (273). How does the Convent transform some of the women of Ruby, even though it is viewed as a haven for evil?

3. **Reverend Pulliam's and Reverend Misner's characters:** What does each reverend represent himself to be, and how does each triumph in his own way?

Writing about the two reverends could lead you to an exploration of the role of Christianity in African-American communities. Rather than simply listing their character traits and beliefs, try to situate each man's role in the ongoing struggle in which the town of Ruby engages. The town faces a major family feud between the Fleetwood and Morgan families, as well as a power struggle between the older generation and the younger generation. The reverends seem to be on either side of the debates taking place, even while they try to forge some sort of reconciliation. Reverend Misner seems to be trying to help people realize the divinity within them, whereas Reverend Pulliam seems steeped in traditional beliefs that God is outside of the worshipper and has the ability and desire to punish those who go against God's wishes. When talking about the people of Ruby, Reverend Misner says they "love [their children] to death" (210). What is he alluding to, and would Reverend Pulliam have made such a comment?

History and Context

One way to explore the riches of *Paradise* is through an exploration of the historical context of the novel. Published in 1997, this was the novel Morrison produced just after winning the Nobel Prize in literature. *Paradise* was considered the third part of Morrison's trilogy, following *Beloved* and *Jazz*. Each novel focuses on a tragic murder and traces the lives of the murdered and the victims, often switching their roles. The novels also expose the aftereffects of slavery and racial prejudice on a community. In an essay, you can explore the historical facts included in the novel as well as the context at the time, such as the reception the novel received because of its complexity. The novel was viewed as extremely complex because the fragmented narrative that coalesces by the end of the story often challenges readers. Looking at *Paradise* in the context of *Beloved* and *Jazz* could also prove helpful when exploring narrative style, the difficulty of a text, and Morrison's allusions to traumatic historical events.

Sample Topics:

1. **All-black towns and the African-American middle class:** In the context of the novel, what is the purpose of an all-black town, and does Ruby fulfill its mission?

   Ruby is known to be "stable, prosperous" and "a deliberately beautiful town governed by responsible men" (277). Examining the irony in these two statements, we can see the deliberate way it was created and the desire of the citizens to have a place where order was of utmost importance. The novel examines the historical context in which African Americans moved upward in society. The fifteen families in the town become mythological and are venerated by the townsfolk, as is evident in the nativity play.

2. ***Beloved, Jazz,* and *Paradise* as a trilogy:** How do the three novels intertwine in terms of their storylines, characterization, and narrative point of view?

   For such a broad topic, a writer may want to pick one of the issues, such as characterization, then narrow the focus to one or two characters, for example. The murders in each of the novels may be a strong starting point, and the community reaction to Sethe's murder of her infant in *Beloved* could be compared to the cover-up of the murders at the Convent in *Paradise.* What determines innocence or guilt in both cases? Both *Paradise* and *Jazz* have epigraphs that are taken from the poem "Thunder, Perfect Mind" from the gnostic manuscripts of Nag Hammadi. You may want to examine the epigraphs and the poem and connect them to themes in both novels.

3. **Historical occurrences such as African-American and Native American alliances, and events such as the effects of Martin Luther King Jr.'s assassination on the American psyche:** What historic events are mentioned in the novel, and how do they impact the characters?

Many historical events are mentioned and could be researched further in an essay. Prohibition, the Vietnam War, color consciousness and discrimination among African Americans are just a few of the historical issues referenced. Each of the topics just mentioned would warrant a fair deal of research; then you could connect the event to the reality of one or two characters, determining the effects of the event on the character.

Philosophy and Ideas

Considering a novel's philosophy and ideas is an interesting way to uncover deeper meaning in the thoughts of characters or the governing ideas of the community, for example. *Paradise* showcases many original terms, such as "the Disallowing," which exposes the historical reality of people being rejected by their own people because of the racism prevalent in society. How do various community members react to this communal memory, and how do some perpetuate the very act that the community denounced? Some ideas in the novel are archetypal, such as the role of disobedience in Christianity. How does Morrison create moments that are unique from conflicts that are not? Other ideas that could be considered in an essay include authority, pride, shame, and the possibility of creating a utopia. Writing about philosophies expressed in the novel might begin by identifying situations that characters face that challenge their worldview. The Steward brothers face the constant challenge of changing traditions, and that idea could be explored through other characters. Who in the novel accepts change and who resists it?

Sample Topics:

1. **The "Disallowing"**: How is the town of Ruby shaped by "the Disallowing" or rejection (194)?

    Writing about the concept of the Disallowing may lead you to investigate the ramifications of this action. The original people who ended up forming the town of Haven in 1890 and then the town of Ruby in 1950 were motivated by the rejection they experienced from the black town members of Fairly, Oklahoma, when they were trying to find a place to settle. Wandering like nomads, they picked up lost children on their journey (Lone was one of the children they found abandoned with her dead mother in the house) and vowed to create a safe haven for themselves. Their rejection "explained why neither the founders of Haven nor their descendants could tolerate anybody but themselves" (13). Why is the concept of rejection integral to the novel's action? Who else is rebuffed in such a fundamental way? What are the ironies of the devastation of the rejection in 1890 and then the ways the residents of Ruby act towards strangers?

2. **Memory and tradition:** How do people uphold tradition in the novel, or struggle against it, and how does their memory play a role?

    Some people in the novel have very clear ideas about the traditions in Ruby, and decide to uphold the traditions in order to save the town. Steward Morgan wonders "If that generation—Misner's and K.D.'s—would have to be sacrificed to get to the next one" (94); in contrast, Reverend Misner wonders whether "past heroism was enough future to live by" (161). Jeff Fleetwood and his cousin Coffee "K.D." Smith had engaged in a gunfight, causing a large rift between the two families, which was supposedly being rectified by K.D. Morgan and Arnette Fleetwood's wedding. The wedding upholds tradition, then Reverend Pulliam's harsh words and Reverend Misner's counterattack of holding up the cross erode any strides toward reconciliation. Patricia Best records the family histories of Ruby and Haven then she burns all her notes, refusing to trace and endorse the traditions any longer. She puts together Ruby and Haven history through "[s]tories about . . . fragments" (188), which is much like the way the novel is put together with fragments of people's lives. The irony about the fragments of family histories is that the point of founding Ruby and Haven was to create a safe haven where people could feel whole.

3. **Disobedience:** What role does disobedience play in the novel? Who struggles with perceived disobedience, and whom are they disobeying?

Billie Delia talks about this concept (150), and it appears elsewhere in the novel in a religious and social context. First examine the context in which disobedience is mentioned then look at the ways conformity plays an important role in the lives of Ruby's citizens. Anyone believed to be a nonconformist is susceptible to negative perceptions by others. Being in control of one's thoughts and actions is also important—many societal norms and standards of behavior apply to women's lives for example, and they are expected to act in a particular way. In what ways are people encouraged to develop religious steadfastness, as Reverend Pulliam says? Why is it so important for the citizens to put God before everything else they do?

4. **Paradise:** What configurations of paradise are there in the text?

The title and references to paradise throughout the text could be viewed literally and ironically. The town that the original nine families create called Ruby is a paradise of sorts. The travelers have been rejected by both blacks and whites and need a place to settle, to feel a sense of belonging. Haven, the next town founded by the fifteen families who descended from the original nine, is supposed to be yet another paradise that people can depend on not to change too drastically, if at all, with outsiders kept at bay. The Convent becomes a paradise for the women and a retreat from the harsh world that metes out abuse to them and ironically becomes the target of the male leaders of Ruby.

Form and Genre

Paradise's form can be a challenge for anyone who wants to write about the novel. The genre is the type of work, in this case fiction, and the form is the structure of the work, in this case a novel told from many narrative voices. In an essay you should look for the many literary devices that the author uses to create and inform the narrative (such as symbols, repetition of words and phrases). What else shapes the novel? How do we get to see into many characters' minds, and what effect does this have on the reader? *Paradise* could be viewed as a text that presents events in a circular rather than linear fashion. The circle as an image is repeated numerous times throughout the text, and is discussed further in the section below. Keep the imagery in mind when discussing the form of the narrative. The novel begins with the murder of the women at the Convent, then returns to that specific moment toward the very end of the novel, furnishing the reader with other nonlinear events in the lives of the residents of Haven and Ruby.

Sample Topics:

1. **The challenging text:** In what ways does *Paradise* challenge the reader?

Many people struggle with the fragmented stories in *Paradise*, and the memories that characters have that need to be pieced together into a history of Ruby and Haven. A writer could focus on areas that are proving difficult for him or her and try to work with those in an essay. Many post-modern novels are not linear, not in chronological order, and not simple. Each section in *Paradise* is named after a woman but does not necessarily give the full story of that character's life. Often the male characters who engage in the attack on the women are described in a woman's section, adding to the complexity of each part.

2. **Point of view:** What is the purpose of the shifts in point of view in the novel?

The many shifts in point of view are interesting, because as noted above, the shift in point of view often provides numerous stories, not just the background of that particular woman. It may also be interesting to discuss in an essay the way the book focuses on female lives, but within the sections on these women there is an abundance of male characters who are fully developed. You can also explore how the sections build on each other, and how we are given more information about an event hinted at many chapters before.

3. **Protagonists and antagonists:** How do the protagonists and antagonists shape the action of the novel?

Identifying antagonists will help you to narrow down your focus for this broad topic. Isolation, death, the vigilantism of the community, certain Christian doctrines of God's wrath, and rejection are powerful antagonists. Antagonists can be forces of nature (like the blizzard that kills the white family) or internal conflicts (like Soane's belief that losing her baby is punishment for going to the Convent). Sweetie and Jeff's child Save-Marie is the first person to die in Ruby. How is this death significant? After the massacre at the Convent, when people are shell-shocked by the events, they think, "How could so clean and blessed a mission devour itself and become the world they had escaped?" (292). Why is the Convent perceived as an antagonist for the rest of the community?

4. **The setting:** How does the setting have an impact on the narratives?

The physical setting is significant and could be examined in an essay on the importance of location to the characters and the narrative. Pay attention to physical descriptions of places and the ways meaning is assigned to location. For example, the fact that the Convent originally belonged to a person that the community of Ruby would judge harshly already provides justification for storming the venue and ridding the town of the imagined wayward women. The journeying that different people engage in that ultimately leads to their freedom in many respects could be included in the discussion on place. Much of the lore about Ruby's ancestors takes place while the townsfolk were journeying—escaping from persecution and following the benevolent urgings of an ancestor figure.

Language, Symbols, and Imagery

An author's language choices for particular characters or moments in the book can reveal a great deal. Look at the way figurative language is used to say something about a concept. Rather than just listing the many symbols in the book, try to imagine what the symbols say about certain situations or people. A lot of the language in the text is connected to religious ideas. Some of the supernatural visions that Connie and others have tell us volumes about the role of Christianity in their lives and their struggle to adhere to Christian ideals in spite of the experiences that they are having. Characters' names often suggest their character, and could be explored in a discussion of language.

Sample Topics:

1. **Figurative language: metaphors/similes/personification/ symbols:** What symbols permeate the text and what do they mean in the context of the novel?

Rather than simply listing symbols, try to decipher what they may be saying about characters, the community, or people's actions. The oven and the garden in the Convent seem to be noteworthy symbols. Both are integral to the action of the novel. The oven provides a social gathering point for the citizens of Ruby, and it becomes the center of a heated debate over its inscription. It represents the struggles that the founding fathers of Haven and Ruby experience and tells the story of "the Disallowing." The youth of Ruby do not have the history burned into their memories the way Deacon and Steward Morgan do, so the youth lose the significance of the oven. The oven represents change, past struggles, and people's ability to overcome extreme misfortune. The garden at the convent also has many religious connotations, and the harvest from the garden becomes an important part of Ruby's culture. Is the garden the safe haven where the Convent women can find shelter from the harsh realities of life?

2. **Imagery:** What examples of circular imagery are present in the novel and what do they suggest?

In writing about imagery, try to identify the pattern of imagery, where the image is repeated, and in what context. Then examine what the imagery might mean in the context of characters' behaviors. The buzzards "circled the town" (147) during K.D.'s wedding to Arnette after a couple and their baby disappear in the blizzard, and "[p]lants grew in a circle" (40) in the convent's garden; these are just two of many circular images in the novel. If *Paradise* is the third of a trilogy, then this novel itself could be part of the circle, maybe suggesting that the events are timeless and there is no real beginning or end to the events in all three novels.

3. **Literal and figurative "seeing":** Explore the ways people "see" literally and figuratively.

Literal seeing and figurative seeing or knowing are present throughout the text with many different characters and in various situations. You could write about eyesight, foresight, and knowledge by focusing on one or two characters who seem to have the ability to see or know truths that others do not. The twins have financial foresight but seem to lack self-knowledge. Deacon engages in an affair with Connie, and it remains ambiguous whether or not he shoots the woman he loved. Connie has spiritual knowledge but her physical eyes fail her, and people find it painful and difficult to even look into her eyes.

4. **Storytelling:** How does the storytelling in the novel impact the various characters?

Writing about the stories that people tell themselves and others might include a look at the various truths that people create for themselves. Characters convince themselves of various truths and hold on dearly to their vision of reality, even though changing times may call for a revision of traditional ways. Deacon and Steward Morgan both tell themselves the stories of the founding of Ruby and Haven, and they are driven to murder to ensure the town of Ruby retains the glory of being an all-black town with little contact with the outside world that it has always enjoyed. The language people use in their storytelling is also important, as is perspective and point of view. From the men's point of view, the women at the Convent are slovenly and threaten the tranquility of Ruby, even though Ruby's citizens have experienced a tremendous amount of pain and loss unrelated to the change that is so vehemently resisted.

Bibliography for *Paradise*

Dalsgard, Katrine. "The One All-Black Town Worth the Pain: (African) American Exceptionism, Historical Narration, and the Critique of Nationhood in Toni Morrison's *Paradise*." *African American Review* 35, no. 2 (2001): 233–48.

Kubitscheck, Missy Dehn. *Toni Morrison: A Critical Companion.* Westport, CT: Greenwood P, 1998.

Mbalia, Doreatha Drummond. *Toni Morrison's Developing Class Consciousness.* 2d ed. Selinsgrove, PA: Susquehanna UP, 2004.

Reames, Kelly. Paradise: *A Reader's Guide.* New York: Continuum, 2001.

LOVE

READING TO WRITE

TONI MORRISON says the following about the characters in *Love*: "The point really is that their struggle is a very human struggle and their effort to become and to remain human is very much based on language, but primarily the effort to love." Morrison's eighth novel brings together numerous themes and conversations that were examined in her earlier books, such as the ways language can serve as a tool of liberation, and the repercussions of abuse. In *Love,* the idea that people can find redemption through love itself is examined. A reader can delight in different examples of love from previous novels, and can enjoy some of the similarities between characters and narrative form in *Love* and other novels. The narrative style of introducing ideas and clues to the reader that have to be unraveled and pieced together (as is the case in *Beloved* and *Paradise,* for example) can also be found in *Love.* As you read carefully for meaning and to examine the author's methods, you may ask yourself how effective this method is and how the reader gains knowledge through the slow revelation of hidden facts, mysteries, and secrets.

Examining a section of the novel and identifying themes, symbols, and the language used will help you in your essay writing. A close reading of the text identifies recurring themes and symbols, for example; then your task is to examine what the symbols mean in the context of the story or what the author is trying to tell us about human nature through the repetition or placement of these symbols. In the following passage, Junior Vivian's childhood abuse by her uncles is revealed:

She stepped out onto the road and had not gone fifty feet when a truckful of uncles clattered behind her. She jumped left, of course, instead of right, but they had anticipated that. When the front fender knocked her sideways, the rear tire crushed her toes.

A bumpy ride in the bed of the truck, a place on Vivian's cot, whiskey in her mouth, camphor in her nose—nothing woke her until the pain ratcheted down to unbearable. Junior opened her eyes to fever and a hurt so stunning she could not fill her lungs. Breath came and went in thimblefuls. Day after day she lay there, first unable, then refusing, to cry or speak to Vivian, who was telling her how thankful she should be that the uncles had found her sprawled on the roadside, her baby girl Junior struck down by a car driven, no doubt, by a town bastard too biggedy to stop after running over a little girl and check to see if she was dead or leastwise give her a lift. (58–59)

A careful examination of this passage reveals many of the novel's themes and techniques used to develop characters. Junior's painful experience is not only physical, but also emotionally wrenching. Other characters experience both emotional and physical pain in their relationships. Junior's physical deformity becomes a source of shame for her, another theme in the novel. She realizes from her uncles' vicious attack and their lies to protect themselves that she is not safe there. She cannot trust her own relatives to care for her. The role of the family in the novel is an important one, and the family is not usually the source of comfort and trust.

People's dishonesty and betrayal is also seen in the novel numerous times, and illustrates dilemmas that people often face in life and sometimes deal with by cheating others. The silence that Junior chooses over telling the truth could be viewed as a survival technique, since her uncles are obviously likely to harm her again. People's silence is referred to many times, and often has severe repercussions. Junior flees from this life of abuse and deceit and ends up in the correctional institute, and is incarcerated for later defending herself against the administrator who tries to sexually molest her. Characters often run away from past pain, although they are not always successful. Vivian, who thinks her "baby girl Junior" was hurt by a "bastard too biggedy to stop" brings up another idea in the novel about class differences. An interesting essay on class status in the novel could lead from a discussion of Vivian's mistaken conclusion that an upper-class man treated her this way, when the act was actually that of her own brothers' treachery.

Many aspects of the novel, such as the way people hurt themselves when they are trying to exact revenge, could be explored at length. The recollections that people have make up the plot of the novel, and these recollections could be examined and connected to characterization, theme, and language, for example. Some of the characters' actions in the novel are morally reprehensible, but as in *The Bluest Eye*, in which the incestuous Cholly Breedlove is not totally demonized, in *Love* the predatory "reprobate" Bill Cosey is also presented in a humane fashion. Central to the action of the novel is the fixation that the femal characters have for Bill Cosey. Others in the community, such as Sandler Gibbons, also seem to live in his shadow, and look up to him.

TOPICS AND STRATEGIES

Here you will find a variety of topics to consider. It is up to you to inter-pret the events and characters in the novel in an original way. Doing your own research can help you to situate some of the occurrences in the novel into historical context and can also help you to identify a unique approach to the novel.

Themes

Writers can identify themes in a work of literature by paying attention to repeated or emphasized words, ideas, or characters' patterns of behavior, since all of these may suggest themes or concepts in the novel. In *Love*, the opening of the book mentions the word silence, and we see it men-tioned in many contexts throughout the novel. Once you have identified a theme, try to uncover what the novel is saying about the theme. With the theme of silence, maybe we could deduce that silence is important to a character such as Junior Vivian. She is punished for her behavior when she fights back against an inappropriate sexual advance made by an administrator at the correctional facility. The witness to the sexual vio-lence is bribed so that he will keep his silence, and Junior ends up being incarcerated for refusing to be silenced. When writing about theme, you may write about connected themes, such as escape and fear, and you may find some of your themes blending with the Philosophies and Ideas sug-gestions that are explored in the later section.

Sample Topics:

1. **Shame:** How does Junior Vivian's shame impact her interactions with others in the novel? Who else suffers from shame about their circumstances?

   Junior Vivian's tragic childhood provides numerous instances of shame that could be used as the basis of an essay. Her dishonest uncles and their cruelty cause her embarrassment about her physical body (because she is ashamed of her crushed foot). Her negative self-image could be related to the humiliation inflicted on the prostitutes in the novel, for example. Writing about the shame that characters or communities of people experience could lead you to a discussion of specific instances such as Heed's and Christine's childhood experiences and the ways the shame transforms into self-hatred and hatred for another person or group of people.

2. **Dishonesty:** Discuss the impact of L's act of dishonesty that is revealed at the end of the novel.

   L believes her deceit is saving the Cosey women from shame and being disowned of their rightful property and inheritance. There are other acts of dishonesty that have far-reaching effects, such as the lies that Junior Vivian's uncles tell. Why is honesty so important to the characters? Do they end up deceiving themselves in their desire to cheat someone else? Is a judgment made of those who withhold or manipulate the truth in order to help others?

3. **Love and hatred:** How do characters express love in the novel?

   The book's title leaves the reader many opportunities to ponder the different kinds of love that characters feel, desire, or try to escape from. An essay could focus on the irony of the title, and the ways that the love that characters express often transforms into hatred. The love in the title is not solely ironic since there are many instances of tender expressions of love. You could also evaluate unconventional expressions of love, such as Romen Gibbons's act of untying Pretty Fay after she had been raped seven times.

4. **Clarity:** How do the reader and the characters achieve clarity by the end of the novel?

Morrison's novels are continually viewed as a challenge for the reader; and *Love* is no exception. You could write about readers and characters gaining clarity. The clarity that May achieves in her insanity is, of course, ironic. What is Morrison saying about the nature of clarity with the example of May's life? In what way *is* May's life clearer when she is insane than before? The events in the novel are slowly revealed to the reader in such a way that previous ideas we have (that the menu is Bill Cosey's will, for example) are clarified by various characters' admissions. How do the careful revelations impact the reader?

Character

Writing about character could include a discussion of character traits, how the author shows us a character is a particular way, and the changes a character undergoes in the course of the novel. Sandler Gibbons focuses on the past, much like many of the characters, and many of the characters' relationship to the past can be assessed in an essay. What is Heed trying to conceal about the past, and why? What has Christine been running away from most of her life? The impact of the community and family on the individual is a major theme in the novel, and can be seen in the actions of the characters and the ways they are characterized—often through another's viewpoint. The readers, therefore, get many perspectives about a character, including L's perspectives on community members. Because some of the characters' behavior can be morally appraised, the reader is often left to evaluate conduct. You can investigate what the characters' actions mean in that specific social context, and how Morrison creates believable characters whose deeds are often morally questionable.

Sample Topics:

1. **Bill Cosey's character:** How is Bill developed as a character who is central to the action of the novel?

   Described early in the novel by Sandler Gibbons as an "old reprobate" and someone who "had a lot to answer for" (17), the reader is at first puzzled by these descriptions of Bill Cosey, the formidable owner of the Cosey Resort who provides jobs and security for many people over a number of years. Soon the reader comes to an awareness of his actions, and it is up to us to unravel why he remains at the forefront of so many people's consciousness and if he deserves these accolades. Vida Gibbons remains convinced he was poisoned, but does not believe he deserved such a fate. Ironically, poisoning does cause Bill's death, which many believe to be a heart attack or heartache. L "admits" to poisoning him with foxglove, which is also known as "Dead Man's Bell's" and "Bloody Fingers" because of its toxicity. She rewrites his will, which she thinks is unfair to the Cosey women, and by this act manages to undermine some of the power he held when alive. What other misfortunes and misunderstandings does L create by reassigning his property from Celestial to the Cosey women in a rather ambiguous way? Because Bill Cosey's character preoccupies the lives of so many of the characters, what do L's actions suggest about his power?

2. **Romen Gibbons's and Junior Vivian's characters:** Why are the "adults" concerned about Junior and Romen having a relationship?

   Junior Vivian's arrival at the beach town of Silk begins one of the novel's many mysteries. The connection that Vivian and Romen share seems to be purely physical and continues while Junior fantasizes about Bill Cosey, whose ghost she sees. Romen Gibbons engages in an internal struggle that involves two prevailing sides of him. His desire to fit in with his schoolmates and his sense of decency seem to battle. Both characters appear innocent but experience alarming realities, and these experiences could be expanded on further in an essay.

3. **Heed the Night Cosey's and Christine Cosey's characters:** At first glance, the relationship between the two is unclear, then the reader slowly gets a sense of their relationship. What is the root of their hatred for one another?

Writing about the way these two characters despise each other would lead you to a discussion of the way their identities unfold slowly. We are told early on that Christine is May's daughter, but it is unclear why Christine is in the house cooking and serving Heed and why Heed is confined to her room. As the truth unfolds Heed's and Christine's reminiscing allows the reader to recreate their stories. Locked in a fierce battle over their right to the Monarch house, each one finds out the importance of the other's love. Christine's multiple affairs, which also define her character, seem to stem from her rejection at an early age, when Bill Cosey chose her best friend Heed as his child bride.

History and Context

One way to explore the riches of *Love* is by examining the historical context of the novel. Morrison's novels are famed for incorporating the historical struggles of African Americans and other groups into the narrative. Morrison often presents the difficulties of historically undermined groups and examines what happens when people's freedoms are denied, their options limited, and their self-esteem crushed. Not only does Morrison include the misfortunes of despised groups, she also illustrates what happens to the oppressor. In *Love*, you may want to consider the various historical figures and events that deeply affect characters. Since much of the conflict involves Bill Cosey and the repercussions of his actions, taking a look at the historical events associated with his character may also be interesting in an essay. Because this is Morrison's eighth novel, you could also consider the story in the context of her other works of fiction. There are some parallels drawn between characters and the narrative structure of *Love* and those in *The Bluest Eye, Sula,* and *Tar Baby,* for example.

Sample Topics:

1. **Women's rights and other historical events:** How does the struggle for women's equality impact the characters' lives in the novel?

   Many of the flashbacks and recollections that characters have occur in the 1940s, '50s, and '60s. Some of the attitudes about women's place in society that people have correlate to the time period and the ways society viewed women's equality. When Christine runs away from home, she ends up at the "boarding house" for prostitutes, and begins to create a sense of self. Christine's multiple abortions also illustrates women's newfound control over their lives (although she has seven abortions, so maybe Morrison is commenting on this extreme example). The song "Ain't nobody's business if I do" by Jimmy Witherspoon that Heed listens to when she has the brief affair with Knox Sinclair (172) speaks volumes about the steps women were taking to live autonomous lives. You could also discuss the role of other historical events mentioned, such as the Great Depression and the GI bill, which also play a significant role in characters' lives.

2. ***Love* in the context of *The Bluest Eye* and *Sula*:** How does *Love* continue the themes of child sexual abuse and women's friendships that *The Bluest Eye* and *Sula* introduced?

   Numerous themes present in *The Bluest Eye* and *Sula* are echoed in *Love*. Doing a comparative study of *The Bluest Eye* and *Love* could lead you to write an essay about the family life of the Breedloves in comparison to the Cosey family that Bill Cosey creates by marrying his granddaughter's eleven-year-old best friend. The similarities between *Sula* and *Love* could be discussed in an essay that focuses on the friendships between Nel and Sula and Heed and Christine. Rather than simply reiterating the nature of each of the friendships, maybe explore what the friendships tell us about women's role in society, or what societal forces cause the strife in the friendships.

3. **The African-American civil rights struggle:** How is the civil rights movement integral to characters' lives?

Integration in general is an important part of the novel. You could explore the role that people believe desegregation plays in the failure of Bill Cosey's resort. The desegregation of war plants is also mentioned and serves to illustrate the social climate that called for acceptance of African Americans in daily life. You could look into the equal rights groups mentioned such as CORE (Congress of Racial Equality founded in 1942), SNCC (Student Nonviolent Coordinating Committee from 1960–66) and various events such as the bus boycotts, voting rights, the Alabama church bombings, and the leaders or people of note during that time like Martin Luther King Jr., Emmett Till, and Malcolm X. Christine and her mother, May, argue about the civil rights movement and the need for African Americans to protest their treatment when her mother asks: "Why can't you all just quiet down?" and Christine retorts "Three hundred years of quiet not enough for you?" (165). This conversation also references the theme of silence in the novel, so you could include a discussion of silence as a way of keeping people oppressed, and the power people wielded by speaking up.

Philosophy and Ideas

Addressing the philosophies in the text is an effective way to assess certain social movements and the beliefs people held at particular historical moments. Some of the concepts you could deal with are racial inequality, the denunciation of certain forms of music, perceived insanity, murder, and people's sense of personal responsibility. The community plays a large role in the characters' lives. What is the role of the community or of witnesses to terrible acts? There are instances in the book when people witness others being treated in an appalling manner. What is Morrison saying about the responses of witnesses? Should they remain silent or should they intervene?

Sample Topics:

1. **Sexual abuse of children:** How does the novel treat the reality of violence against girls?

   Because of the way Heed's marriage to Bill Cosey when she is eleven is revealed to the reader, we are unaware for some time that child sexual abuse is at the center of the plot. Not only can you write about the actual relationship between Cosey and Heed, but you can also discuss the way the narrative is constructed deliberately to keep the reader in the dark for a long time. What is the effect of this narrative withholding? How does the relationship inform us about Bill Cosey's character in ways that contradict the manner in which L and Vida Gibbons describe him? Can Cosey be described as purely positive or negative? Why would Morrison make his character so morally complex?

2. **Speculation:** In what ways does speculation play a role in the ways characters view others?

   Heed, Sandler Gibbons, and Junior all engage in speculating about other characters. Writing about this idea could lead you to discuss how certain characters figure each other out, the methods they use to learn about a person, and the plans they create to maybe even manipulate that person. Who is successful in learning about other characters and their motives? Whose manipulation is successful?

3. **Class:** Why is the Johnson family looked down upon, and what are the results of the community's attitudes toward them?

   Writing about Heed the Night Johnson Cosey and the way she and her family are perceived by others may lead you into a discussion of the ways people distinguish class in the novel. People from various Beaches and sides of town and people with particular careers are treated in ways that relate to their class status. Heed's class status renders her particularly vulnerable, and because of her family's financial lack, Bill Cosey's proposition becomes attractive. This essay would probably also include the way girls are treated (see above), since Heed's class and gender seem to intersect and put her in the position of being "sold" by her family to Cosey.

Language, Symbols, and Imagery

An author's language choices can reveal a lot about particular characters or events in the book. Look at the way figurative language is used to say something about a concept. Rather than just listing the many symbols in the book, try to imagine what the symbols say about certain situations or people. In *Love,* the character's lives seem to revolve around Bill Cosey. Each chapter is named after the relationship he has to a particular character, and the way that character idolizes or idealizes him. You could examine what he represents for each person, and why he manages to become the central focus of many women's lives. Look at the ways each woman remembers him, the imagery used to describe him, or the language used in conversation about him. Lack of language, or silence, is another important theme. How does language often fail characters? How does silence condemn, lead to further pain, or liberate characters?

Sample Topics:

1. **Figurative language: metaphors/similes/personification/symbols:** War imagery is repeated throughout the novel. What do the examples that you find seem to suggest?

   The Vietnam War is mentioned briefly, as well as wars that people engage in, like the one that rages between Heed and Christine Cosey. You could examine the effect in the story of the two family members engaging in a battle that lasts decades. You may also refer to the way the war is revealed to us, and how pieces of the picture finally come together to create the final story and the truth, shame, and betrayal involved in the relationship the girls shared.

2. **The language of L's commentary:** How does L's italicized commentary frame the action of the novel?

In an essay about L's commentary, you could focus on the language itself and how her vernacular affects the reader. The way she tells her stories is significant—the reader can feel a sense of ease because of the conversational tone, and the reader trusts her perspective. Does L always come across as a trustworthy narrator? At one point in the novel, she is described as a peacekeeper who "would take no-one's side" (133). Was it her responsibility to take sides? How does she eventually come to Heed's aid? Some of the themes involved in her commentary include the role of the past in shaping people's lives, the way life has changed (not necessarily for the better), and the expectations of women in society. She also believes in the Police-heads who are responsible for the drowning deaths of various holiday goers. How does her matter-of-fact conversation about and belief in these mythical beings shape the reader's view of her?

3. **Conversation:** How do people come to terms with their lives and their pasts through conversation?

L tells us "how precious the tongue is" (201). Exploring the various conversations that people engage in and the ways their language can have a major impact on another person could lead to an interesting essay. The conversation that Christine and Heed engage in is a dreamlike one that evokes the conversation between Beloved, Sethe, and Denver in *Beloved.* In the conversation that Heed and Christine have, they come to terms with their tragic childhoods and forgive each other for the abandonment that each experiences. Where else in the text is the tongue precious, and how does conversation affect other characters?

Compare and Contrast Essays

Comparing and contrasting elements in a literary work can help to illuminate what these differences or similarities mean in the larger context of the novel. Be sure that the essay does not deteriorate into a list of similarities and differences. Try instead to connect the similarities and differences to what the novel is saying about a particular theme or idea. You could compare and contrast ideas, characters, or narrative structure between *Love* and other novels if there is some basis for the comparison or contrast. An analysis of love in *Love* and *Sula,* for example, may reveal a fascinating discovery of the unique conditions faced by Christine Cosey and Sula as they try to assert themselves as individuals. The stark contrasts and similarities between the various expressions of love in different novels could also be explored.

Sample Topics:

1. **Compare character experiences in *Sula* and *Love*:** What anguish do characters in *Sula* and *Love* experience?

   Love presents the reader with many of life's painful ironies, such as L's comment that "traitors help progress" (139). You could use this quotation as a starting point for an essay on the way that adversity affects characters in the town of Medallion in *Sula* and the town of Silk in *Love*. Rather than listing characters and their painful experiences, maybe limit your exploration to two characters whose anguish seems memorable. The tedium that seems to control characters such as Nel Wright in *Sula* and Christine Cosey in *Love* could be an interesting focus for an essay. Imagine what Morrison is saying by illustrating their pain. Is their distress brought about because of reluctance to go against social norms or because of their inability to imagine their lives in any other ways? How does each character finally break away from his or her pain, or is escape impossible?

2. **Compare narrative form in *Love* and *Beloved*:** How does *Love* echo some of the narrative forms in *Beloved*?

   There are many similarities between these two novels to consider. One focus may be to explore the character development, another to look at the ways the narrative voice reveals facts to the reader. The manner in which the two stories unfold is fascinating and could produce an interesting essay that includes a discussion of dramatic irony (when the reader is aware of information that a character is not). You could examine the information that the reader is given about certain characters that the characters might not know. At what point do the readers "know" about Beloved? Do we ever really know if she is a ghost? Do we know for certain that the Narrator L is alive? What effect does the ambiguity have on the reader?

3. **The community versus the individual:** Discuss the individual's desire for autonomy, in opposition to the community's influence in *Love*.

Love has many contrasts within the plot. One significant contrast explored is the way the individual sees him- or herself, versus the role of the community in assessing and evaluating that person. A character such as Bill Cosey could make for an interesting study in an essay. You could evaluate the different portrayals and assessments of his character and decide which seem to be the most credible. Does anyone in the novel have a monopoly over the truth? L mentions truth many times, and it is often the case that people frequently feel that they hold the true perspective about a certain event or person. How do community members remember Bill Cosey, and what are some of the positive and negative traits that they feel he exhibited?

4. **Contrast the family in *Love* to the family in other Morrison novels:** How does Morrison portray the family in *Love* in contrast to another novel?

In *The Bluest Eye* and *Love*, family dysfunction is at the core of the narratives. The way that family trouble is revealed to the reader could be the focus of an essay. You could consider the immediate family woes that the reader sees in *The Bluest Eye* and contrast that to the slow revelation of facts that expose the terrible secret in *Love*. You might focus on the children themselves and how they view the world around them. How are Cholly Breedlove and Bill Cosey, the two perpetrators of child sexual abuse, characterized and described? How do they function as heads of the household, and how do the adult women in the novel respond to them? What roles do they play in the lives of the children they have harmed? You may also want to consider the commentary that Morrison is making about the family: In *The Bluest Eye*, the Breedloves contrast with the Dick and Jane family, and in *Love*, the narrator L concedes that "families make the best enemies" (139).

Bibliography and Online Resources for *Love*

Morrison, Toni. Radio interview with Tavis Smiley Oct. 2003. *Tavis Smiley Show*. National Public Radio. Retrieved 20 Jan. 2007 <http://www.npr.org/templates/story/story.php?storyId=1484643>.

Thomas, Valorie D. "Placing Toni Morrison's 'LOVE': African American and Women of Color Feminists Theorizing Embodiment, Home, and Memory as Political Resistance," *The International Journal of the Humanities* (2006).

INDEX